"Karin Holsinger Sherman has written a beautiful exposition of my books. By identifying an underlying, nonviolent 'question of being,' she has united their themes in a deeply perceptive way. I am grateful to her for her work."

—James Douglass, Catholic Worker,
Founder of Mary's House and Ground Zero Center for Nonviolent Action

"Karin Holsinger Sherman presents [Douglass's] prophetic insights . . . [and] skillfully applies Douglass's 'Ontology of Nonviolence' to address this latest threat [of global warming]. This book is a great companion to the republishing of the classic works of James, our prophet. Many thanks."

—Louis Vitale, OFM, Pace e Bene Action Advocate

A Question of Being

A Question of Being

The Integration of Resistance and Contemplation in James Douglass's Theology of Nonviolence

Karin Holsinger Sherman

Wipf & Stock
PUBLISHERS
Eugene, Oregon

A QUESTION OF BEING
The Integration of Resistance and Contemplation in James Douglass's
Theology of Nonviolence

Copyright © 2007 Karin Holsinger Sherman. All rights reserved. Except for brief quotations in critical publications or reviews, no part of this book may be reproduced in any manner without prior written permission from the publisher. Write: Permissions, Wipf and Stock, 199 W. 8th Ave., Eugene, OR 97401.

Cover painting, Medieval Scene, by John L. Sherman, 2006. www.johnshermanart.com. Used by permission.

ISBN 13: 978-1-55635-144-0

Manufactured in the U.S.A.

*Dedicated to my parents Don and Ruth
and to my husband Jake*

*"Resistance and contemplation,
sunlight and darkness,
one Way, one God-man Liberator,
a single roaring flame,
a question of Being . . . "*

James Douglass

Contents

Acknowledgments xi
Introduction xiii

1: The Life and Historical Context of James Douglass 1

2: The Community of Influence 21

3: Themes and Theology: Douglass's Cross and Kingdom 47

4: An Ontology of Nonviolence:
The Uniting of Contemplation and Resistance 83

5: Conclusion: Constructive Engagements
with James Douglass's Theology of Nonviolence 97

Bibliography 109

Acknowledgments

THIS BOOK has been more gift than labor, and I am deeply grateful to those whose support and encouragement have brought it into being. First and foremost, I would like to thank Jim Douglass, whose gift to this book extended far beyond the powerful words and thoughts that inspired it. His gracious reception of the original thesis, the time spent correcting it and providing further material, and his kind words and encouragement have made this printing possible. It has truly been an honor to know and receive support from a person such as Jim. I am grateful for my editor, Jim Tedrick, and for the others at Wipf & Stock who believed enough in the value of Jim's message to reprint his four beautiful books and to follow with this one. I am also indebted to Fr. Joe Chinnici, whose invaluable guidance throughout my thesis work went beyond the call of duty. Four others also deserve special thanks for their inspiration and assistance in the initial development of this work in thesis form: Lisa Fullam, Fr. Louie Vitale, Clare Ronzani, and Bruce Lescher. And to the Franciscan School of Theology as a whole I offer my heartfelt thanks. There are few places that encourage spiritual growth alongside academic learning, and that do it in such an inviting and authentic way.

I offer my deep gratitude to those whose gift of Christian community made the writing of this book a pleasure—fellow students and friends at St. Jerome's, and the women of EE whose embrace of the sacrament of justice and peace continues to inspire me. To Amy Schultz and the Nevada Desert Experience for the opportunity to experiment with truth and for bringing Douglass's words to life. To the Sherman family, for their support, enthusiasm, and for teaching me the value of contemplation. And to my family, for their infinite stream of encouragement and for instilling in me the values of compassion, justice, and peace, I am thankful beyond words. This thesis is merely an extension of my parents' own lives and their embrace of nonviolence. Finally, to my husband I offer my deepest gratitude, for editing, for cheering me on, and for showing me that love is a sacrament, the world pregnant with God.

Introduction

IN THE new forward to James Douglass's *The Non-Violent Cross*, Ched Myers writes that the book "represents the first full-fledged attempt to forge a nonviolent 'theology of revolution and peace,' and as such, remains a landmark for faith-based struggles for social change."[1] Considering James Douglass's position as one of the first to articulate a nonviolent theology, it is surprising how little has been written on his work over the last few decades. Fortunately, this dearth of secondary material has not restricted the influence of Douglass's books. Indeed, with Wipf & Stock's new reprinting of his four major works, one realizes just how significant his work has been for figures like Stanley Hauerwas, Robert McAfee Brown, Philip and Daniel Berrigan, John Dear, and Walter Wink, among so many others. It is therefore a great honor to provide an exploration into the nonviolent theology of James Douglass, and to place myself among those men and women who have been profoundly influenced by his writings.

I first encountered Douglass as an undergraduate at Whitworth College, when my professor of Peace Studies, Dr. John Yoder, assigned *The Nonviolent Coming of God* as course reading. Unfortunately, as I had not yet developed an interest in spirituality, nor could remotely fathom the idea of sacramentality, I read the book and then put it aside. As one of those trying to change the world from the 'outside,' I only understood Douglass's thought inasmuch as I could use it for a debate on Christian pacifism.

Thankfully I encountered Douglass again, this time as a student at the Franciscan School of Theology at the Graduate Theological Union in Berkeley. A Mennonite with a strong deontological bent, I had found myself challenged by the discovery of the Catholic contemplative tradition and was awakened to the possibility of spiritual disciplines as much more than mere means to an end—morning drills to help develop Christian muscle—but formative encounters with God. There seemed to me to be a powerful, ontological relationship between spirituality and social justice, contemplation and action; yet, among all of the theological treatises in the seminary library, none were able to articulate this relationship in a manner

---

1. Ched Myers, "Forward," in James W. Douglass, *The Non-Violent Cross* (1968; reprint, with a new forward by Ched Myers, Eugene, OR: Wipf & Stock, 2006).

that satisfied my deepest intuitions. And I was not alone—a number of my fellow seminarians were also searching for a more integrated understanding of the intertwining of spirituality and active work for peace and justice. I especially wanted to better understand the integral connection between spirituality and action in the environmental arena, having found in my previous work a powerful connection between spiritual discipline and a more robust environmental ethic.

In a course entitled "Spirituality and Liberation," taught by Jesuit School of Theology professor Clare Ronzani, I was introduced again to James Douglass's work and his ability to articulate the deeper connection between the spiritual life and social involvement. While Thomas Merton was also influential for me, I found that Douglass's condensed interpretation of Merton's thought streamlined the integration of contemplation and action. After exploring his writings and discovering in his work an "ontology of nonviolence," I recognized a theology that could speak to seminarians and activists alike. Douglass presents a theology that is vital for healing the divisions created by the Martha/Mary syndrome in our churches, where spirituality is relegated to the private sphere and has nothing to say about the way we practice justice and peace. Perhaps more importantly, it is a theology that speaks to a world that still flounders under terrible acts of violence and bears the weight of the tasks that lie before us.

Unlike most seminarians who choose to write on a particular theologian, I had the wonderful privilege of working with a contemporary who is still engaged in the process of writing and is actively involved in the ongoing struggle for peace and justice. His life attests to that which he articulates and as such, gives tremendous force to the ideas within his books. More than a series of theological treatises, his written works testify to his lived experience of the nonviolent Kingdom.

What I attempt to do in the following pages is explore how, through a strongly incarnational theology that focuses on the themes of suffering and the Kingdom, James Douglass creates an ontology of nonviolence that is able to unite the frequently divorced themes of resistance and contemplation. In order to do so, I have found two methodological approaches helpful. I first use a historical approach to situate Douglass's thought in his broader cultural, religious, and political context. Here I focus specifically on those trajectories which most directly impact Douglass's integration of contemplation into his theology of nonviolent resistance. A consideration of Douglass's major intellectual and exemplary influences is equally vital to situating Douglass historically and introducing us to his thought. In

Introduction

the second place, I employ what one could call a systematic and developmental hermeneutic, as I pay attention to the chronological development of Douglass's works as a whole. This method will help to clarify the coherencies within Douglass's thought that his style of writing often failed to make explicit. In the process we necessarily touch on those theological and philosophical matters with which Douglass was concerned.

In order to best analyze Douglass's thought, I adhere to primary sources in explicating his theology, looking primarily at his four main books, as well as articles published between 1963 and 1981, the time period in which contemplation entered into his thought and maintained a strong presence. Some of these articles were graciously shared with me by Douglass himself, who was also very generous in discussing his life and work with me in early February of 2005 and in the Spring of 2007. Because these interviews were informal, I do not quote from them explicitly, though they have helped to shape my interpretation of Douglass's thought.

As mentioned earlier, while a number of works which trace the development of the American Christian peace movement make reference to Douglass, little has been written specifically on Douglass and his thought. Charles A. Curran dedicates a chapter to explicating Douglass's ethics in his book *American Catholic Social Ethics* which, like my own work, finds Douglass's Christology and eschatology to be the key components of his thought. Kenneth Preston's thesis, "Seeking the Reign of God: James Douglass's Theology of Nonviolence," also contributes greatly to an analysis of Douglass's work by tracing his understanding of nonviolence over the course of his major writings.[2] Although I refer to these two works, this book does not focus on Douglass's nonviolence or ethics *per se*. Rather, it explores his nonviolence in light of its integration of spirituality and political and social involvement.

The structure of the book is as follows. Chapter I examines Douglass's biography and three historical trajectories: the fusion of Christianity and American nationalism in the early Cold War period; the emergence of cultural critique in the late fifties and early sixties and the Catholic pacifist tradition; and the post-1972 period of disillusionment. The second chapter considers the lives and thought of Dorothy Day, Mahatma Gandhi, and Thomas Merton, as well as their unique intellectual and exemplary influence on Douglass's own ideas. In Chapter III, we explicate the themes

2. See Charles E. Curran, *American Catholic Social Ethics: Twentieth-Century Approaches* (Notre Dame: University of Notre Dame Press, 1982). See also Kenneth Preston, "Seeking the Reign of God: James Douglass's Theology of Nonviolence" (MA Thesis, Graduate Theological Union, 2001).

of the Cross and the Kingdom as they developed chronologically in Douglass's writing career. In the fourth chapter, we draw from the previous chapters to show how Douglass creates an 'ontology of nonviolence.' By then considering the significance of contemplation to such an ontology, we demonstrate how such an ontology provides a cohesive integration of resistance and contemplation. Finally, in the fifth chapter, we will conclude with a critical engagement of Douglass's work in order to show areas where it may be improved upon, as well as to explore its continuing relevance and lasting importance.

Paying attention to the requirements of space, elegance, and the narrow scope of this book, there are, of course, numerous conversations and explorations that had to be left untouched. In light of our focus on the nexus of resistance and contemplation, I only briefly explore Douglass's emphasis on nuclear disarmament, a major facet of his overall project. I also do not treat Douglass's Biblical exegesis which constitutes the bulk of his 1992 work *The Nonviolent Coming of God*. This later work, which reflects a further evolution of Douglass's nonviolent theology, also deals with his later experiences in Birmingham, the influence of Martin Luther King, Jr., and an increased interest in issues of race and poverty. While certainly deserving of further treatment, these developments tend to fall just outside of our area of concern. Douglass's role in helping to formulate the Second Vatican Council's documents on war, and his early arguments against deterrence are also outside of the scope of this book. For similar reasons I have not dealt with Douglass's current project which involves a sustained investigation into the assassinations of John F. Kennedy, Martin Luther King, Jr., Malcolm X, and Robert Kennedy. Further exploration into all of these areas is certainly called for, as is Douglass's overall influence in the history of the American peace movement.

1

The Life and Historical Context of James Douglass

As with any writer and thinker, James Douglass's thought did not develop in a vacuum. The turbulent political and social climates of the twentieth century provided the ecology for Douglass's experiences and ideas, and the resulting development of his nonviolent theology. As we will see, nearly all of Douglass's major intellectual and exemplary influences were twentieth-century figures, a fact which elucidates Douglass's grounding in his own historical situation. In addition, Douglass's increasing interest in the spiritual component of nonviolence, which is of particular interest to our purposes here, owes itself to the changing historical context of the latter half of the twentieth century.

Douglass's thought, however, was not merely informed by his contextual experience and left to develop on its own through intellectual discourse or analytical reasoning. His thinking was inextricably linked with his own involvement in society, as a peace activist and contemplative. Experimenting in his own life with his ideas regarding a theology of nonviolence, Douglass allowed his lived experience to continually challenge and evolve his thinking. Because of this deeply intertwined relationship between Douglass's experience and thought, any extended treatment of his work must begin with a broader understanding of his life and times.

We will begin with a brief exploration of Douglass's biography, followed by a consideration of the historical context that shaped Douglass's thought. It is not our intention here to provide a thorough analysis of twentieth-century political and social movements, but rather to identify the major trajectories that significantly molded Douglass's ideas regarding contemplation and social involvement. We will treat three such trajectories: the fusion of Christianity and American nationalism in the early Cold War period; the emergence of cultural critique in the late fifties and early sixties and the Catholic pacifist tradition; and the post-1972 period of disillusionment. By exploring first these historical influences on Douglass's life, we will then be able to examine more thoroughly Douglass's thought.

A Brief Biography

James Douglass was born in the Similkameen Valley of British Columbia, Canada in 1937 to American parents. A dual citizen, Douglass received his early education from Catholic elementary and high schools in the United States. In 1955, he enrolled at the University of California at Berkeley. After a mere two months, and with the military draft in effect, Douglass chose to enlist in the Army, serving six months at Fort Ord in California. Following this period of service, he attended Santa Clara University in an attempt to discover his Catholic identity, receiving his B.A. in English from the Jesuit school in 1960.

At Santa Clara, a number of relationships and encounters had a marked influence on the direction Douglass's life would take. Role models Clayton and Myra Barbeau, for example, showed him what it looked like to commit oneself fully to the reign of God, relying totally on the economics of Providence while raising a growing family. An early interaction with Dorothy Day challenged Douglass to examine his own conscience and question his involvement in the Army Reserves. The Jesuit professor, Father Austin Fagothey provided challenging opposition to Douglass's stance against nuclear war, and in doing so, pushed Douglass to a more critical development of his own position.[1]

After graduating from Santa Clara in 1960, Douglass went on to receive his Masters of Theology from Notre Dame University two years later. His interest in the relationship of affirmative and negative theologies, in immanence and transcendence together, can already be witnessed in an early published work the following year in *The Downside Review*.[2] Noting that the topic of nuclear war had been neglected by theologians, Douglass traveled to Rome to work towards his doctorate at the Gregorian University in 1962. After a year of studies, he felt it imperative to work

---

1. For a more detailed discussion of these influences, see Preston, "Seeking the Reign of God," 23–27. For his own account of the influences of Day and Fagothey, see also James W. Douglass, *The Nonviolent Coming of God* (1993; reprint, with a new forward by Jonathan Wilson-Hartgrove, Eugene, OR: Wipf & Stock, 2006), 98–104.

2. See James Douglass, "The Negative Theology of Dionysius the Areopagite," *The Downside Review*, no. 81 (1963): 115–24. In the article, Douglass explains the coexistence of both affirmative theology and negative theology in Dionysius' works. He understands the full mystical experience as a paradoxical encounter with the transcendent God who is then embraced in his creation.

full-time contacting and assisting bishops at the Second Vatican Council on the subject of war and peace in *The Constitution on the Church in the Modern World* (later to become the conciliar document, *Gaudium et Spes*). He collaborated in "the peace lobby" with Dorothy Day, Eileen Egan, Gordon Zahn, and Hildegard and Jean Goss-Mayr during their various trips to Rome, and with Thomas Merton and Daniel Berrigan in their letters and appeals to bishops. The Council responded by condemning total war and supporting conscientious objection in *Gaudium et Spes*. This experience with the bishops and the prevalence of the just war ethic would have a significant place in his first book, *The Nonviolent Cross*, published several years later.

After returning from Rome in 1965, Douglass taught for a year at Bellarmine College in Kentucky. His encounter with Merton at this time, along with their subsequent friendship and correspondence tremendously impacted Douglass's thought and life.[3] In 1966, Douglass moved to British Columbia to write *The Nonviolent Cross* (1968). After its completion, he taught at the University of Hawaii between 1968 and 1969, shortly becoming involved with a number of students in the formation of the Hawaii Resistance. Although Douglass initially opposed civil disobedience, he participated with the students in a blockade of National Guard trucks, "moved," he said, "by the Holy Spirit."[4] The experience with Hawaii Resistance and the two weeks he spent in prison for civil disobedience were formative for Douglass, and he dedicates the second part of his book *Resistance and Contemplation* to the Hawaii Resistance. In addition, Douglass's second wife, Shelley, had a profound influence on him during this time, teaching him "more deeply than even Merton and the Berrigans what the contemplative dimension of resistance means."[5]

In his acts of resistance in Hawaii, Douglass was brought back to "the need for a deeper base, or for a rock outside the world on which to stand."[6] He withdrew with his wife to British Columbia to write and to seek the meaning of *metanoia*, resulting in his second book, *Resistance and Contemplation*, published in 1972. Douglass writes of this period in a later book:

---

3. For Merton's letters to Douglass, see Thomas Merton, *The Hidden Ground of Love*, ed. William H. Shannon (New York: Farrar, Straus, Giroux, 1985), 159–67. We will examine Merton's influence on Douglass in greater detail in the following chapter.

4. Preston, "Seeking the Reign of God," 30.

5. James W. Douglass, *Resistance and Contemplation: The Way of Liberation* (1972; reprint, with a new foreword by Elizabeth McAlister, Eugene, OR: Wipf & Stock, 2006), 10.

6. James Douglass, "Non-Violence and Metanoia," *Katallagete* 5, no. 2 (1974): 29.

A Question of Being

> My world over the ten years, 1966–75, was really two worlds, a world of resistance and a world of contemplation. The two worlds existed on opposite sides of a border, dividing the United States and Canada, the two countries in which I am a citizen.
>
> On the U.S. side of the border, my life was one of resistance—resistance to the war in Indochina, to the global policies the war expressed, and to a deeper spirit of death in America. This world of resistance to killing was experienced mainly in Honolulu, Hawaii, as a member of two resistance communities....
>
> The other world I knew, on the Canadian side of the border, was a world of contemplation. I have always returned to my original home... to work through questions of evil, violence, and nonviolence which have opened to truth only through a sustained period of struggle, and of writing through the stages of the struggle.[7]

Douglass returned to Hawaii to teach in 1972, this time joining the nonviolent resistance community, catholic Action of Hawaii. One of the more significant actions during this period took place at the Hickam Air Base at the Pacific Air Force Headquarters where Douglass, along with two others, poured blood over top-secret warfare files. The action resulted in prison time and a drawn-out court case, but had more significant repercussions for Douglass's own spiritual and personal life. Although Douglass called the action a "miraculous event," it also "opened up a darkness in myself which is a deeper need for *metanoia* all over again."[8]

In 1978, Douglass moved with his wife Shelley to Silverdale, Washington, to continue a Gandhian campaign of nonviolent resistance (begun in January 1975) at the Bangor Trident submarine base. They had formed the Ground Zero Center for Nonviolent Action in 1977, a campaign based on the principles of Gandhi's *satyagraha* and the teachings of Christ and Martin Luther King, Jr. Although the goal was to stop Trident, Douglass understood the process to be more important than the goal. Thus, over the next few years, the Ground Zero community worked to raise the awareness of both the base personnel and the local community through demonstrations, and worked to unite people through leafleting, dialogue, and the development of mutual respect.[9]

In 1983, Douglass completed his third book, *Lightning East to West*, a spiritual journal of sorts that explores the great power of the "kingdom

---

7. James W. Douglass, *Lightning East to West: Jesus, Gandhi, and the Nuclear Age* (1983; reprint, with a new afterword by John Dear, Eugene, OR: Wipf & Stock, 2006), 66.

8. Douglass, "Non-Violence and Metanoia," 29.

9. Preston, "Seeking the Reign of God," 59.

of Reality" and spiritual nonviolence. Eight years later he published *The Nonviolent Coming of God* (1991), after he and Shelley moved to Birmingham, Alabama. There they opened Mary's House, a Catholic Worker house of hospitality, in 1992. Throughout the 1990s, Douglass embarked on nonviolent missions to places such as Israel, Palestine, Sarajevo under siege, Belgrade, Rome and Iraq. He continues to be active within the Catholic Worker community and is involved in an extensive writing project on the assassinations of the Kennedys, Malcolm X, and Martin Luther King, Jr.

The Historical Context

Having briefly outlined James Douglass's biography, we must now turn to the historical events surrounding his life. Only by understanding the historical context that shaped his experience and informed his thought can we also understand how his theology of nonviolence evolved towards an ever deeper integration of contemplation and resistance. We will consider three historical trajectories in the twentieth-century that are most relevant for our purposes here: the Cold War with its nuclear proliferation and Christian sanction, the rise of socio-cultural criticism and the correlating Catholic peace tradition, and finally, the diminished optimism and disillusionment among resistance movements after 1972.

The Cold War, Nuclear Proliferation, and Christian Nationalism

The world into which James Douglass was delivered in 1937 was one plagued by violence. Although Douglass was a young boy during the Second World War, he would be keenly aware later in life of the atomic bombing of Hiroshima and Nagasaki and the obliteration bombing of cities such as Dresden. For a number of Americans the experience of dropping such destructive weapons revealed the harsh and dreadful reality of new technologies. Such bombings, along with the later threat of nuclear annihilation in the Cold War, led to an increased sense of apocalypticism after World War II. Although apocalyptic thought had often pervaded the Christian worldview with its varied eschatological doctrines regarding the world's violent and impending demise, the end of the Second World War made such doctrines increasingly real. According to Paul Boyer, "In the aftermath of Hiroshima and Nagasaki . . . such prophetic biblical passages as 'The heavens shall pass away with a great noise, and the elements shall melt with fervent heat, the earth also and the works that are therein shall be burned up' (II Peter 3:10) took on a chilling resonance."[10] Eschatology was renewed in the consciousness of theologians who took very seriously the possibility of an imminent end. Although apocalyptic expectations numbed some, it led to a renewed vigor for social justice among others.

Not all Americans sensed the apocalypse. However, as the conflict between the United States and the Soviet Union reached its height, not in open war, but in tense ideological opposition and growing stockpiles of weapons of annihilation, overwhelming fear was pervasive among the American public. The nuclear proliferation of the Cold War and the atmospheric tests of such weapons permeated the American consciousness, shaking the sense of safety, stability, and even survival. The issue of nuclear weapons pushed its way into the center of American culture in the mid-1950s. Recent events such as the Bikini tests (1946–1963), Chicago's radioactive rain (1955), Russia's nuclear experiments, and increased civil defense drills renewed the fear of radioactive fallout.[11]

This period of nuclear fear and consequential activism came to an end in 1963 when, after the Cuban missile crisis of 1962, the U.S., Britain, and the Soviet Union agreed to ban atmospheric testing. As Stewart Alsop viewed it in 1967, "In recent years there has been something like a conspiracy of silence about the threat of nuclear holocaust."[12] This period of what Boyer calls the "Big Sleep" was not due, however, to a diminished nuclear threat.[13] On the contrary, the number of nuclear warheads in the United States remained above 24,000 between 1963 and 1980, and more nuclear weapons were tested in the five-year period after the test ban treaty than in the five years prior.[14] Boyer gives the credit for this "Big Sleep" to other factors: the illusion of diminished risk, a loss of immediacy, the complexity and comfort of the deterrence theory, and the absorption by the Vietnam War of activists' energy.

Although most Americans succumbed to complacency regarding nuclear proliferation after 1963, James Douglass remained highly active around nuclear issues. This may have been due to his long fight against the idea of deterrence as well as a refusal, perhaps, to believe that "technocrats could be counted on to 'manage' the nuclear arms competition while radi-

---

10. Paul Boyer, *By the Bomb's Early Light: American Thought and Culture at the Dawn of the Atomic Age* (Chapel Hill: University of North Carolina Press, 1994), 237.

11. Ibid., 352.

12. Stewart Alsop, "MIRV and FOBS Spell DEATH," *Reader's Digest* (July 1968): 134, quoted in Ibid., 355.

13. Ibid., 356–58.

14. Ibid., 356.

cals turned their energies elsewhere."[15] He would be at the Ground Zero Center, when, in the late 1970s, the nuclear issue reemerged with a new focus on nuclear power and in 1980 with the accession of Ronald Reagan to the presidency. This resurgence of the nuclear debate helped to spur the National Conference of Catholic Bishops to issue a pastoral letter in 1983 entitled *The Challenge of Peace*, calling on Christians to reconsider how natural law and Christian teaching speak to the morality of nuclear weapons and their use in American foreign policy.[16]

Prior to 1983, however, and particularly before the Second Vatican Council in 1963, the Church had frequently sent what was, at best, ambiguous messages regarding the morality of nuclear weapons. It is to the silence of the Church and its entrenchment with governments that Douglass spoke in his earlier writings, and so it is to the "capitulation" of the Church that we now turn.

Although Douglass's Catholicism was a fundamental part of who he was, he was troubled by the complicity of the Church in the wars and injustices of the twentieth century. Indeed, "in the first half of the twentieth century the church achieved a position of prominence, of Constantinian alliance with power and authority that characterized the era of the two world wars and their aftermath."[17] The shift in the position of the major Catholic peace organization, founded in 1927, reflected this reality. The Catholic Association for International Peace (CAIP) viewed peacemaking as the domain of international agreement and top-down governmental action. Initially, the CAIP favored American neutrality and criticized excessive nationalism on the part of Catholics.[18] However, as the nation itself moved away from neutrality, the CAIP also came to favor the theory that collective military security most effectively serves peace.[19] The association

---

15. Ibid., 359.

16. National Conference of Catholic Bishops, *The Challenge of Peace: God's Promise and Our Response* (East Orange, N.J.: Advocate Pub. Corp., 1983). For a thorough, if more conservative reading and critique of the letter, the Just War, pacifist traditions, and the evolution of episcopal thought, see James E. Dougherty, *The Bishops and Nuclear Weapons* (Hamden, CT: Archon Books, 1984).

17. Ronald G. Musto, *The Catholic Peace Tradition* (Maryknoll, NY: Orbis Books, 1986), 238.

18. An influential member of the CAIP, C. J. H. Hayes' wrote a pamphlet critiquing Catholics for too easily subordinating their own religious principles to anti-foreign nationalism. See Carlton Joseph Huntley Hayes, *Patriotism, Nationalism and the Brotherhood of Man; a Report of the Committee on National Attitudes, [Catholic Association for International Peace] Pamphlet; No. 25;* (New York: Paulist Press, 1937).

19. Patricia F. McNeal, *The American Catholic Peace Movement* (New York: Arno Press,

relied heavily on the just war theory and supported, without question, the U.S. foreign and military policy as a means to collective security. It went so far as to suggest moral guidelines that justified the use of atomic weapons. As Ronald Musto explains, "peace through accommodation to U.S. power was CAIP's central policy—even through the war in Vietnam—until its demise in 1967."[20]

Such unquestioning support of American policy was not limited to the CAIP, but extended, rather, to a great deal of American Christian culture. During this period the symbolic language of religion became tightly coupled with American national identity in the major denominations.[21] A firm connection had been built between the principles of democracy, the moral life, social stability and religion. The church combined its two fronts against secularism and communism, linking the restoration of God in public society to modern capitalism. The 1952 statement by the Catholic Bishops of the United States, entitled "Religion, Our Most Vital National Asset," illustrates well the integration of religion and American loyalty during this period. In extolling the unifying and patriotic benefits of education in Christian schools, the document states, "The differences which are harmful to our country are those which divide our people in their duty of loyalty, patriotism and good citizenship." According to the bishops, instruction in religious schools inculcates the duties of loyalty and civil service.[22] Indeed, as society witnessed a revival among religious groups, "the ideological argument engendered by the war laid the foundations for the unique mixture of denominational upsurge and Cold War culture that exalted the 'American way of life,' anti-communism, and a family-centered domestic ideology."[23]

Douglass called into question this uncritical support of American political decisions during the Cold War—what he considered the entrenched church. He found his views articulated in Carl Amery's work, *Capitulation* (1967), which critiqued German Catholicism for its capitulation to the "milieu." Criticizing theologians for "blindly following the prejudices of

---

1978), 29–30.

20. Musto, *The Catholic Peace Tradition*, 241.

21. Joseph P. Chinnici, "The Catholic Community at Prayer, 1926–1976," in *Habits of Devotion: Catholic Religious Practice in Twentieth-Century America*, ed. James M. O'Toole (Ithaca: Cornell University Press, 2004), 53.

22. Catholic Bishops of the United States, "Religion, Our Most Vital National Asset," *Catholic Action* 34, no. 12 (1952): 5.

23. Chinnici, "The Catholic Community at Prayer, 1926–1976," 53.

their milieu,"[24] Amery exposes how cultural homogeny and the celebration of middle-class virtues of diligence, cleanliness, punctuality, etc. become hindrances and distortions of the gospel message. Looking particularly at the inability of German Catholicism to resist the rise of Nazism, Amery blames the milieu for "its dependence on leaders, its distrust of historical initiatives, and its instinctive conception of the Christian life as a collection of prescriptions and values. . . ."[25]

Dorothy Dohen's examination of the fusion of religion and nationalism, *Nationalism and American Catholicism*, was published in the same year as Amery's *Capitulation*. Seeing American Catholics as eager to conflate the cause of Communism with the cause of Christ, Dohen argued that the Catholic nationalism of her time (in the fifties and sixties) used religion to sanction nationalist goals (as contrasted with earlier forms of Catholic nationalism that did the reverse).[26] Francis Cardinal Spellman of New York, for example, would not voice any criticism of the bombings of Hiroshima and Nagasaki and was additionally silent on the nuclear issue. For Dohen, the American Catholic hierarchy's silence on the question of obliteration bombings served as a clear symptom of Catholicism's union with nationalism.[27] More revealing was Spellman's answer to the question of the United States' involvement in Vietnam when he said he fully supported everything it does: "My country, may it always be right. Right or wrong, my country."[28] Although there were some bishops who dissented from American policy,[29] David O'Brien points out that such church leaders were a minority, while in 1965 Spellman's forceful defense of American involvement in Vietnam was closer to center.[30]

The unquestioning devotion of Christians to the American national agenda in the 1950s and early 1960s began to dissipate in the latter half of the decade, as Douglass was writing *The Nonviolent Cross*. In 1965, the Tet

---

24. Carl Amery, *Capitulation: The Lesson of German Catholicism*, trans. Edward Quinn (New York: Herder and Herder, 1967), 19.

25. Ibid., 43.

26. Dorothy Dohen, *Nationalism and American Catholicism* (New York: Sheed and Ward, Inc., 1967), 171.

27. Ibid., 154. See also McNeal, *The American Catholic Peace Movement*, 108.

28. Dohen, *Nationalism and American Catholicism*, 1.

29. A statement issued by nine bishops in 1965, for example, applied the Second Vatican Council's condemnation of total war. See *Continuum* (Summer 1965), inside cover.

30. David J. O'Brien, "American Catholic Opposition to the Vietnam War: A Preliminary Assessment," in *War or Peace? The Search for New Answers*, ed. Thomas A. Shannon (Maryknoll, NY: Orbis Books, 1982), 125.

offensive altered general opinion and saw increased Catholic opposition to the war. Such opposition was reflected in the appearance of mild reservations towards the war on the part of bishops. According to O'Brien, it was Spellman's strong remarks in 1966 which referred to the war in Vietnam as "a war for civilization," that signaled the end of the staunch episcopal support for the war:

> While criticism and dissent remained muted and isolated, the bishops seemed to realize in the wake of Spellman's controversial statement, which would have been unexceptional in earlier wars, that this was a new war and a new time, and public moral commentary would have to be seriously considered and carefully stated.[31]

Indeed, the 1968 pastoral letter, "Human Life in Our Day," while remaining neutral, questioned whether the Vietnam War could still be considered a just war.[32] In the following years, anti-war statements became increasingly common. In 1971, the United States Catholic Conference conclusively answered the just-war question, stating: "It is our firm conviction therefore that the ending of this war is a moral imperative of the highest priority."[33]

As we have seen, the nuclear threat and Christian nationalism that existed in the period between World War II and the end of the 1960s set the stage for Douglass's early work on nonviolence. In subsequent chapters, we will witness this influence in his apocalyptic tone, as well as in his call for Christians to return to the margins, through the way of the cross. This trajectory, however, reveals only one of the historical contexts influencing Douglass's thought. Equally influential were the socio-cultural critiques and movements which emerged as a powerful force in the sixties, and had their roots in the previous decades. Their impact on the Christian peace movement which so profoundly influenced Douglass makes them worthy of note.

The Rise of Socio-Cultural Criticism and the Catholic Peace Tradition

James Douglass both participated in and was influenced by the surge of cultural and political criticism in the 1960s. This surge can be attributed

---

31. Ibid., 126.

32. *Human Life in Our Day: A Collective Pastoral Letter of the American Hierarchy Issued November 15, 1968*, (Washington, D.C.: the Conference, 1968).

33. *Resolution on Southeast Asia: November, 1971*, (Washington, D.C.: United States Catholic Conference, 1971). Quoted in O'Brien, "American Catholic Opposition to the Vietnam War: A Preliminary Assessment," 130.

to a number of factors. Young radicals like Douglass were no doubt influenced by the generation before them who had become more conscious of the problems of war, race, and poverty in the 1930s, problems which resurfaced with great force in the 1960s.[34] In addition, cultural criticism was abetted by the dissolution of a national purpose. As the fifties came to a close, the church was no longer able to tie together its common enemies of secularism and communism. The end of the Korean War in 1953, the censure of Joseph McCarthy in 1954, and the death of Stalin in 1958, for example, all diminished the domination of the enemy in American thought. As Chinnici notes, "by 1960 there was a growing awareness that the national consensus or 'purpose' had collapsed."[35] When Americans could no longer rally behind the fear of their common enemies, the public mood changed to one of cultural critique.

Sharp critiques of American institutions and policies also emerged as many began to recognize the tremendous gaps between the ideal American culture touted in the previous decades and a starker reality. As Charles Curran explains: "A generation who had been trained to think of America as the citadel of freedom, equality, fairness, and peace now began to see the great disparity between these ideals and the realities of the 1960s."[36] As Americans emphasized that the nation's ideals match reality, they increased their demand for structural change. According to Chinnici, public discourse was beginning to be shaped by alternative internal critiques; issues relating to racial prejudice, equal opportunity, and poverty surfaced in the place of anti-communism.[37]

The civil rights movement provides an apt example of this internal critique. With the civil rights movement gaining momentum in the fifties, it had become increasingly apparent that racial discrimination was deeply ingrained in American culture, shedding light on the myth of America as a "land of opportunity." In addressing their own needs, black activists turned to a reinvention of their own culture, questioning the political legitimacy of the liberal model of individualism and free enterprise. As a result, the movement challenged American culture and its deeply held ideas about political behavior.[38] The Black Power movement would intensify this critique in the later part of the 1960s and into the following decade.

34. Charles E. Curran, *American Catholic Social Ethics: Twentieth-Century Approaches* (Notre Dame: University of Notre Dame Press, 1982), 233–34.
35. Chinnici, "The Catholic Community at Prayer, 1926–1976," 74.
36. Curran, *American Catholic Social Ethics: Twentieth-Century Approaches*, 234–35.
37. Chinnici, "The Catholic Community at Prayer, 1926–1976," 74.
38. David R. Colburn and George E. Pozzetta, "Race, Ethnicity, and the Evolution

The issue of poverty, too, challenged political legitimacy and American culture. Increasing attention to the effects of United States' economic colonialism coupled with an awareness of the plight of the nation's poor made the material prosperity and seemingly limitless possibilities of the previous decade appear as little more than a panacea. The poverty movement of the sixties, like the black and ethnic movements, questioned whether structures and institutions were in fact barriers to justice. Other issues, too, such as feminism, youth culture, and American military involvement overseas challenged the complicity of institutions in the prevailing systems of injustice and called traditional cultural authority and political legitimacy into question, as new centers of authority, such as universities, television, and corporations, subverted local centers of power.[39]

James Douglass experienced this institutional skepticism as a young student and theologian. He was a member of a generation that, through their own participation in political and social structures, learned to question the legitimacy of such institutions, especially the Church.

> They knew the social encyclicals of Pope Pius XI and also the restraints of the post-World War II world, its containments and its presuppositions about the compatibility of religious practices and the American way of life. They experienced the benefits of higher education and often perceived at first hand the fault lines of gender differentiation, racism, and poverty that cut through the Cold War consensus.[40]

Carried by the rapidly changing times, this new generation participated in the revitalization of the church and the growing emphasis on peace. Indeed, the sixties witnessed a rejuvenation of Catholicism, as it broke from the past to renew its structures and spirituality. Aware of their ability to challenge the entrenched church and frustrated by an increasingly disastrous war in Vietnam, many from Douglass's generation joined with a Catholic Pacifist tradition in its critique of the structures of violence. Like the civil rights movement, however, the Catholic peace movement did not begin in the 1960s. Its origins reached back several decades to the creation of the Catholic Worker movement.

---

of Political Legitimacy," in *The Sixties: From Memory to History*, ed. David Farber (Chapel Hill: The University of North Carolina Press, 1994), 121.

39. David Farber, "Introduction," in *The Sixties*, ed. David Farber (Chapel Hill: North Carolina University Press, 1994).

40. Chinnici, "The Catholic Community at Prayer, 1926–1976," 85.

The Catholic pacifist movement, which existed contemporaneously with the non-pacifist CAIP, in essence began under the leadership of Dorothy Day (1897–1980) and Peter Maurin (1877–1949) in the Catholic Worker movement. The Catholic Worker emphasized a commitment to both social justice and nonviolence, speaking out against the just war tradition and on behalf of conscientious objection. The Catholic Worker (and Christian Peace Fellowship later) practiced a "radical evangelism" that saw peace as "a dynamic process and a personal commitment to the pacifism of the gospels. It starts with individual conscience and conversion and then works to change institutions."[41] Although Day encountered much criticism for her adherence to pacifism, the Catholic Worker's commitment to its nonviolent ideals laid the groundwork for resistance to war in the following decades. We will examine this Catholic Worker movement and its influence on Douglass in greater detail in the following chapter.

Pacifism was indeed an unpopular stance before and during World War II; however, with the atomic bombing of Hiroshima and Nagasaki, and the obliteration bombing of German cities during the war, increasingly moderate voices began to join in the dissent. A moral theologian at Fordham University, John C. Ford, for example, condemned such obliteration bombings and called into question the concept of the just war.[42] In the 1950s, anarchist Ammon Hennacy helped increase the resistance to the annual Civil Defense drills with members of the Catholic Worker. His additional protests against military headquarters and hydrogen bomb testing in Nevada helped to spread the message and support for nonviolence. The 'peace movement,' however, was still barely audible at this time as popular opinion swung in favor of the heightened Cold War and Korean War. According to McNeal, "By 1950, only despair remained among the peace remnant."[43]

Ronald G. Musto emphasizes the importance of the year 1962 for Catholic peacemaking. In Chicago, a Conference on Christian Conscience and Modern Warfare faced the problem of nuclear war (even though the conference was unable to clarify a moral direction). In addition, the lobbying group PAX reemerged to pursue change in official church attitudes on war. In 1964, the founding of the Catholic Peace Fellowship, led by Thomas Merton (1915–1968) and Daniel Berrigan (1921–), signaled the new force of nonviolence in the Catholic Church. The Church hierarchy

---

41. Musto, *The Catholic Peace Tradition*, 238.
42. See Ibid., 246. and McNeal, *The American Catholic Peace Movement*, 109.
43. McNeal, *The American Catholic Peace Movement*, 183.

began to reflect the changing times as well. Major shifts had already taken place in papal thought with Pius XII (1939–1958) who recognized the futility of modern war and insisted that the only way to prevent war was through controlled bilateral disarmament.[44]

It was his successor, John XXIII, however, who acknowledged this change and provided a new answer to the question of modern war. Musto asserts that Pope John's encyclical *Pacem in Terris* (April 11, 1963) made explicit the revolution in Catholic thinking on the issues of peace and justice.[45] In the encyclical, John XXIII invokes the rights of individual conscience, emphasizing that not every leader deserves steadfast obedience. In addition, the document's strong criticism of the arms race, as well as its moral judgment on war appears to call the just-war rationale into question.[46] As a result, the document was understood by many, including James Douglass, to advocate a position of nonviolence. It was *Pacem in Terris*, along with the intervention of PAX lobbyists that had the greatest influence for peace at the Second Vatican Council.

The Second Vatican Council, with its creation of the *Pastoral Constitution on the Church in the Modern World*: *Gaudium et Spes* (Dec. 7, 1965), was a significant event for Catholics such as Douglass who were deeply concerned with the issues of modern war and nonviolence. While peace lobbyists may have been disappointed that the Council did not condemn the weapons of modern war themselves, they could not completely disapprove of the new attitude the Catholic hierarchy had adopted in its evaluation of war.

---

44. See Pius' Christmas messages (1939–1942) such as his 1939 appeal for peace, *Un'Ora Grave*: "It is by force of reason, and not by force of arms, that justice makes progress. . . . Nothing is lost with peace; all may be lost with war." Quoted in Harry W. Flannery, ed., *Patterns for Peace: Catholic Statements on International Order* (Westminster, MD: Newman, 1962), 76. A number of Pius' statements and letters emphasize the horror of war and limit the right of war to defense from attack alone. See Stephen E. Lammers, "Catholic Ethics and Pacifism," in *War or Peace? The Search for New Answers*, ed. Thomas A. Shannon (Maryknoll, NY: Orbis Books, 1982), 96.

45. Musto, *The Catholic Peace Tradition*, 188.

46. The strength of John XXIII's disapproval of modern war can be witnessed in the following statements: "Justice, then, right reason and humanity urgently demand that the arms race should cease . . . that nuclear weapons should be banned. . . ." Cited in William J. Gibbons, *Pacem in Terris. Peace on Earth; Encyclical Letter of His Holiness Pope John XXIII* (New York: Paulist Press, 1963), 39. We also find the strong assertion that "it is hardly possible to imagine that in the atomic era war could be used as an instrument of justice." (Gibbons, *Pacem in Terris. Peace on Earth; Encyclical Letter of His Holiness Pope John XXIII*, 43.). It is this latter assertion that Douglass interprets to mean no form of war may be justified. *Pacem in Terris* is therefore a key document for Douglass's justification of his own nonviolent theology. See Douglass, *The Non-Violent Cross*, 84.

The Council both rejected the idea of deterrence, one of the key modern doctrines of defensive war, and provided an official statement on conscientious objection, the first explicit sanction of a pacifist position in Catholic teaching.[47] As a consequence of the Council's document on modern warfare, as well as the influence of the Catholic Worker and the Catholic peace movement, the just war tradition slowly lost its normative value for Catholics. *Gaudium et Spes* and Vatican II signified a tremendous change in the church and opened the door for further movements towards peace.[48]

Vatican II and the momentous changes in the sixties gave significant momentum to the Christian peace movement. Indeed, with the intensification of the Vietnam War in the early 1960's and the implementation of the draft, many found a new encouragement for conscientious objection and a new peace ethic. The Catholic Peace Fellowship (CPF), which Douglass helped to conceive in 1964 with Daniel Berrigan and James Forest, devoted itself to opposing the draft and ending the Vietnam War. Unlike PAX, which was founded in 1962 by Dorothy Day and Eileen Egan and worked for selective conscientious objection within the legal system, the CPF chose to employ protest tactics outside of institutional structures. Similarly, the Catholic Worker continued with its tactics of protest: David Miller, for example, a Catholic Worker, was the first to burn his draft card as a sign of resistance in 1965. Such protests signaled a greater acceptance of civil disobedience by the peace movement.[49] Fathers Daniel and Philip Berrigan came to be seen as the figureheads of this movement, with their involvement in direct action raids and commitment to antiwar activism. The Catonsville Nine action of 1968, in which the Berrigan brothers and

---

47. The Council addresses conscientious objection in Chapter V of the *Pastoral Constitution on the Church in the Modern World*: "It seems just that laws should make humane provision for the case of conscientious objectors who refuse to carry arms, provided they accept some other form of community service." *Church in the Modern World*, paragraph #79, in Austin Flannery, ed., *Vatican Council II, the Conciliar and Post Conciliar Documents*, New rev. ed., *Vatican Collection; V. 1;* (Collegeville, Ind.: Liturgical Press, 1992), 989.

48. For analyses of the place of Vatican II in changing Catholic attitudes towards peace, and the Second Vatican Council's relationship to the American peace movement, see Musto, *The Catholic Peace Tradition*, 191–93.; McNeal, *The American Catholic Peace Movement*, 193–206.; and J. Bryan Hehir, "The Just-War Ethic and Catholic Theology: Dynamics of Change and Continuity," in *War or Peace? The Search for New Answers*, ed. Thomas A. Shannon (Maryknoll, NY: Orbis Books, 1982).

49. A number of these activists, such as James Forest and Daniel Berrigan were initially wary of the tactic of direct action raids and civil disobedience (Curran, 239). James Douglass was likewise opposed to such actions at first. However, as we will see in later chapters, direct action and civil disobedience became extremely significant in his understanding of nonviolence.

seven other Catholics burned draft files with homemade napalm, brought media attention to these actions and highlighted the emergence of the Berrigans as "architects of a new political and theological movement."[50] Labeled the leaders of the "Catholic Left" by the media, the Berrigans began what would become a nationwide movement of nonviolent direct action, with numerous symbolic actions occurring between 1969 and 1972. James Douglass was a leader and participant in such acts of symbolic civil disobedience and was himself inspired by the work of Daniel and Philip Berrigan.[51]

James Douglass was simultaneously the product of and participant in cultural shifts that were taking place in the 1960s. On the broader level, the socio-cultural critiques of the previous decade strongly influenced his willingness and ability to call the Church and government into question. More specifically, the growing Catholic pacifist tradition with its evolving understanding of nonviolence contributed to Douglass's preoccupation with nuclear issues, the Cold War and Vietnam War, and the broader theme of gospel-centered peace. Just as important to Douglass's theology of nonviolence, however, were the events which followed the Catholic resistance movements during the Vietnam War. The demise of the peace movement was to have a significant role in bringing the contemplative element to bear heavily on Douglass's nonviolent theology.

After Vietnam: A crisis of confidence

As previously discussed, in the early 1960s the attention of peace activists had turned from nuclear issues to the escalating war in Vietnam. Television brought the horrors of the war into American homes, as did the institution of the draft. The general peace movement expanded as many saw the deaths of conscripted friends and family members in Southeast Asia as futile and without meaning. The Catholic peace movement joined with the larger movement against the war, which would later experience rifts over issues of effectiveness and political rhetoric. Yet towards the end of the war, the greatest challenge was a profound sense of hopelessness that pervaded the cultural backdrop in the United States. Both the Vietnam War

---

50. McNeal, *The American Catholic Peace Movement*, 241.

51. For more on the Catholic Left and the Berrigans, see McNeal, *The American Catholic Peace Movement*, 241–99. The preface to his book *Resistance and Contemplation* reveals Douglass's indebtedness to the Berrigans. The book, he writes, "is an effort to hear more deeply Dan's and Phil's good news of resistance, and is therefore dedicated to them"(9). For Douglass's own analysis of the Catonsville Nine action, see *Resistance and Contemplation*, 81–84.

and the disillusionment of the late 1960s helped to concretize Douglass's nonviolent thought.

Douglass saw the Southeast Asian nonviolence movements as models of strength from a people entirely committed to peace. In contrast, Douglass criticized Americans for their half-hearted commitment to nonviolence, given only to periodical mass marches and occasional civil disobedience.[52] This "half-hearted commitment" may have been one of a number of factors that contributed to the demise of the peace movement. The end of the war, divisions within the movement itself, and the loss of prominent leaders all gave rise to a period of inaction and disillusionment among resisters. As the war in Vietnam drew to a close in the early 1970s, the American peace movement lost its rallying point and became relatively inactive. As with Douglass, Musto credits the thinned ranks of the Catholic peace movement to a dearth of commitment:

> [R]elatively few of the Catholics who participated were willing to undergo the radical personal conversion that peacemaking required. Thus with the end of the war, considerations of politics, personal career, and fashion drew the majority of those opponents of the war back into the mainstream of American culture and its indifference to matters of peace and justice.[53]

Self-criticism, too, caused a fractioning of the movement. After directing a number of their own peace actions, including the last major rally at the Federal Courthouse in New York City in the fall of 1965, religious pacifist groups joined the broader antiwar coalitions. As the actions intensified over time under the leadership of these general antiwar groups, many participating Catholic pacifists began questioning their tactics. The Vietnam War was grinding on with relatively little public support, and a number in the movement experienced a crisis of faith in the effectiveness of nonviolent action. Some of the Berrigans' followers, for example, went underground in order to launch a revolution. According to O'Brien, "the resistance appeared to push toward the limits of nonviolence, asking how far one could go without crossing the threshold to violence. The awful immediacy of the war and the sense of urgency aroused by the daily destruction of human life, made them less patient than their predecessors with defeat, more determined to end the war, no matter the cost."[54] Fearing that

---

52. Douglass, *Resistance and Contemplation: The Way of Liberation*, 37.
53. Musto, *The Catholic Peace Tradition*, 257.
54. O'Brien, "American Catholic Opposition to the Vietnam War: A Preliminary Assessment," 138.

the emphasis on effective action diminished the gospel witness of nonviolence, many Christians questioned the validity of their own participation in these movements.[55]

The real challenge to the peace movement, however, lay in the emotional state of the broader American culture of the time. In the early 1960s, three major figures, Martin Luther King, Jr., John F. Kennedy, and Robert Kennedy had provided Americans with a tremendous hope for the future. As Farber writes, they gave people "the sense that the nation was about big things and grand possibilities."[56] For many, these three men embodied a faith in social progress and the goodness of humanity. Yet with the deaths of both Martin Luther King, Jr. and Robert Kennedy in 1968, following the death of John F. Kennedy in 1963, the American spirit of idealism was crushed. Douglass writes of this crisis in *Resistance and Contemplation*:

> Americans whose faith in social change passed through the commitments and assassinations of the '60's are afraid that they have already gone too far in, and many have retreated. They have already seen and experienced too much of the world's truth, while a succession of dead leaders and widening slums and wars have ended an earlier vision.[57]

The lack of commitment that Douglass had emphasized earlier was evidenced in this 'retreat' of American activists. The spirit of optimism that had characterized the momentous changes of the decade and the faith in strong leaders such as King and the Kennedys reneged under a new leaderless landscape that could no longer provide a vision for which to strive. In his treatment of this difficult period, Douglass cited Jack Newfield's memoir of Robert Kennedy:

> Now I realized what makes our generation unique, what defines us apart from those who came before the hopeful winter of 1961, and those who came after the murderous spring of 1968. We are the first generation that learned from experience, in our innocent twenties, that things were not really getting better, that we shall *not* overcome. We felt, by the time we reached thirty, that we had already glimpsed the most compassionate leaders our nation could produce, and they had all been assassinated. And from this time

---

55. Musto, *The Catholic Peace Tradition*, 257.

56. David Farber, "The Torch Had Fallen," in Beth Bailey and David Farber, ed., *America in the Seventies* (Lawrence, KS: University Press of Kansas, 2004), 9.

57. Douglass, *Resistance and Contemplation: The Way of Liberation*, 48.

forward, things would get worse: our best political leaders were part of memory now, not hope.[58]

Although it may be argued that the movements of the '60s, rather than dissolving, were institutionalized and absorbed into the cultural fabric, the perception of utopian failure remained. What had once been an eschatological vision of a new world order changed into an apocalyptic pessimism. It was a despair that continued well into the 1970s, and even beyond. William Graebner described it as a "'crisis of confidence,' a loss of faith in the future that was at least in part rooted in the 'wounds' of the past," including the assassinations of the '60s, Watergate, the failure of Vietnam, and economic dislocations.[59] Deflated expectations had led to an 'existential boredom' in the '70s that lay heavy over the country. While some analysts blamed affluence and consumerism, many others, like Graebner, "underscored boredom's roots in a profound and elemental crisis of meaning, values, standards, purposes, and ideals, a crisis reflected in the position and posture of boredom in which nothing mattered. . . ."[60] Many Americans met this existential crisis and postmodern doubt by turning to religious fundamentalism. Others, like Douglass, decided to look critically at the bustling activity and consequences of the previous decade, and turned to a more contemplative search for meaning. Indeed, while Douglass himself reflected the apocalypticism of the times, he did not fully succumb to believing in an inevitable dystopia. For him, the despair of the generation was a necessary antecedent to renewal.

Conclusion

As we have seen, several historical currents are vital in understanding the formation of Douglass's thought. The Cold War period, with its apocalyptic tone and fusion of Christianity and American nationalism developed Douglass's own apocalyptical tenor and strong critique of domesticated Christianity. The emergence of cultural critique in the late fifties and early sixties and its parallels with the Catholic pacifist tradition continued to inform Douglass's institutional critique, as well as providing the role models for his own acts of nonviolent resistance. Finally, the diminished optimism and disillusionment among resistance movements after 1972 provided the

58. Jack Newfield, *Robert Kennedy: A Memoir* (Bantam Books: 1970), 378. Cited in Douglass, *Resistance and Contemplation: The Way of Liberation*, 49.

59. William Graebner, "America's Poseidon Adventure: A Nation in Existential Despair," in Farber, ed., *America in the Seventies*, 157.

60. Ibid., 161.

impetus for Douglass's turn inward, toward the roles of kenosis, contemplation, and conversion in the nonviolent life.

Having explored the broader historical context of Douglass's life and work, we may now turn to those particular people whose influence on Douglass resonates loudly throughout his writings. Dorothy Day, Mahatma Gandhi, and Thomas Merton serve as the three most significant intellectual and exemplary influences on Douglass's thought. By connecting their lives and ideas to his own experience Douglass is able to unite resistance and contemplation in his formulation of an ontology of nonviolence. In order to appreciate fully these aspects of Douglass's thought, we must first explore the rich influence of Day, Gandhi, and Merton.

2

The Community of Influence

As we have seen, James Douglass was deeply immersed in his times, internalizing the apocalypticism of the fifties with the institutional critique of the sixties. These broad movements shaped Douglass's life and thought in crucial ways. Within the turbulence of these movements we can identify at least three significant figures who emerged as primary influences on Douglass's thought regarding the integration of contemplation and action: Dorothy Day (1897–1980), Mahatma Gandhi (1869–1948), and Thomas Merton (1915–1968).[1] Their influence can be witnessed not only in the resonance of their ideas with those of Douglass, but also in the visible presence of the figures themselves throughout Douglass's works. While Day served essentially as an exemplary influence, Gandhi and Merton held tremendous intellectual sway over Douglass's formulation and articulation of nonviolence.

In order to explore the extent to which Day, Gandhi, and Merton affected Douglass, we will consider each figure in his/her own right. By examining in particular their thought regarding nonviolence, spirituality, and resistance, we will better understand Douglass's own formulation of a theology of nonviolent resistance. In terms of Dorothy Day and Thomas Merton, we will also investigate how their personal relationships with

---

1. Few people would be able to narrow their influences to only three people, and Douglass is certainly no exception. A lifetime of learning, dialogue and cooperation with other theologians and activists give his thought a complexity that goes beyond a simple elaboration of Gandhian nonviolence, for example. Martin Luther King, Jr. deserves mention as a profound influence, as does John Howard Yoder. While in Rome, Douglass poured over the pamphlets which would later become Yoder's *The Politics of Jesus*, and the two would later meet and correspond over Douglass's *The Non-Violent Cross*. However, because neither Yoder nor King is as prominent in the works where Douglass first draws together contemplative spirituality and prophetic involvement, we have not included them in our discussion here. I have instead chosen to focus on Day, Gandhi, and Merton, not because they enjoy any sort of exclusive influence on Douglass, but because of their prominence in Douglass's major works and their relevance to Douglass's development of an ontology of nonviolence.

Douglass served to influence his thought. Let us begin by exploring the initial and exemplary influence of Dorothy Day.

Dorothy Day

Born in 1897, a generation before Douglass, Dorothy Day's work grew not from Cold War apocalypticism, but from the growing concern for class equality and workers' rights that was prevalent in the early twentieth century. Early in her life, Day was aware of the great injustices suffered by the lower classes. Highly influenced by Marx, she wrote for a Socialist paper in New York and participated in anarchist groups prior to her conversion to Catholicism. Initially, Day believed the Christianity of her times to be incompatible with her love of the masses—she considered it a comfortable opiate that left the social order unchallenged. When, after giving birth to her daughter, Day was baptized into the Catholic Church, she worked to reconcile the tradition and her growing spirituality with her deep compassion for the poor and marginalized. "How I longed to make a synthesis reconciling body and soul, this world and the next," she wrote in her autobiography.[2]

In 1933, with the help and profound influence of Peter Maurin (1877–1949), Day founded what came to be called the Catholic Worker, a movement primarily centered around a paper for the workers that served to spread Catholic concern for structural injustice. The realization of Maurin and Day's vision soon grew to include numerous Houses of Hospitality (where the poor received help for their basic needs), round-table discussions, and farming communes that also served as retreat centers. As Day describes it in her autobiography, the program was a long-range one, "looking for ownership by the workers of the means of production, the abolition of the assembly line, decentralization of factories, the restoration of crafts and ownership of property."[3]

Although most well-known for her work with the poor and marginalized, Dorothy Day also served as one of the greatest figures in the Catholic Peace Movement. According to Ira Chernus, "For nearly a half a century, she was the most famous, most influential, and most energetic voice proclaiming that Catholics could and should be nonviolent, precisely because they are Catholic."[4] Day led the way in Catholic opposition to World War

---

2. Dorothy Day, *The Long Loneliness: The Autobiography of Dorothy Day* (San Francisco: Harper San Francisco, 1997), 151.

3. Ibid., 220.

4. Ira Chernus, *American Nonviolence: The History of an Idea* (Maryknoll, NY: Orbis

II, a highly unpopular position at that time, by protesting and voicing her opinion in the *Catholic Worker*. Although this decision resulted in a massive drain of support for the *Worker* (subscriptions fell almost seventy-five percent by the end of the war), Day stood firm in making the Catholic Worker a pacifist organization.[5] Day participated in numerous peace and justice movements, two examples of which serve to demonstrate her commitment to nonviolence.

While Catholic Workers had long since practiced fasting, leafleting, and picketing, their embrace of Gandhian nonviolence grew to a new level in 1954 when Day, Ammon Hennacy (1893–1970) and several other Catholic Workers defied the Civil Defense Act by refusing to take shelter during the New York City air raid drill. The following year, Day and Hennacy, along with 28 others including non-Catholics, repeated this act of civil disobedience and were sentenced to five days in prison. Every year thereafter, they refused to participate in these preparations for war, their numbers growing to two thousand by 1960. These protests served as the starting point for increasing political resistance to nuclear weapons in the following years.[6]

Day's commitment to nonviolence was also revealed in her presence at the Second Vatican Council. She led a group of women in prayer, fasting, and dialogue with the Church hierarchy in an effort to obtain a condemnation of nuclear weapons in Council documents. Recognizing the broader repercussions of the arms race on global poverty and hunger, Day "offered my fast in part for the victims of famine all over the world."[7] Her witness was a spiritual compliment to the political lobby of Catholics such as Douglass, who greatly valued her presence at the gathering.[8] As seen in these examples, a radical embrace of nonviolence, along with struggles for worker's rights and justice for the poor would characterize the rest of Day's life.

The theme of nonviolence was embedded in much of Day's philosophy and lived experience. Her emphasis on nonviolence was based in her

Books, 2004), 145.

5. Ibid.,156. For an excellent history of the Catholic Worker movement and its involvement in the peace movement, see the chapter entitled "The Catholic Worker and Peace" in Mel Piehl, *Breaking Bread: The Catholic Worker and the Origin of Catholic Radicalism in America* (Philadelphia: Temple University Press, 1982), 189–239.

6. McNeal, *The American Catholic Peace Movement*, 186–8. See also Chernus, *American Nonviolence*, 157.

7. Robert Ellsberg, ed., *By Little and by Little: The Selected Writings of Dorothy Day* (New York: Alfred A. Knopf, 1984), 332.

8. For Douglass's own description of Day's presence in Rome during the Council, see *The Nonviolent Coming of God*, 101–2.

Christian faith, encompassing both her work for social justice and her resistance to war. A pacifist in her younger years as well, her conversion to Catholicism provided an enhanced understanding of nonviolence drawn from the rich traditions, Scriptures, and social orientation of the Church, including its emphasis on spiritual and corporal works of mercy. In order to fully grasp Day's understanding of nonviolence, we must first examine the significance of personalism and voluntary poverty for Day and the Catholic Worker movement.

Personalism

Day was profoundly influenced by the personalism of Emmanuel Mounier (1905–1950) and Jacques Maritain (1882–1973). This philosophy, which flourished in the mid-twentieth century, held the person to be center of value and meaning in all spheres of life. As Joseph Amato explains:

> Committed to the primacy of the person as a free and spiritual being, personalism denied all attempts to reduce the human being to any immanent order of society, politics, and history. Committed to the person as an embodied and communal being, personalism equally denies all doctrines that deny man's temporality and historicity in the name of a transcendent order.[9]

This personalism emphasized both the infinite worth and profound responsibility of every human being. By living out his belief in personalism, Peter Maurin convinced Day that such was the way of the saints and the path to societal transformation. Maurin and Day thus developed their own distinct version of personalism in the common life and relentless works of mercy of Catholic Worker communities, communities that sacrificed comfort and privilege in recognition of the dignity of those whom society so often rejects.

Personalism, essential to both the personal and social transformation embraced by the Catholic Worker, went hand in hand with Day's emphasis on nonviolence as a way of life.[10] The prioritization of the person above ideology, efficiency, and even effectiveness meant that the larger goal was often subordinate to direct actions of witnessing to the truth, whether

---

9. Joseph Amato, *Mounier and Maritain: A French Catholic Understanding of the Modern World* (University: University of Alabama Press, 1975), 13.

10. See Patrick G. Coy, "Beyond the Ballot Box: The Catholic Worker Movement and Nonviolent Direct Action," in William Thorn, Phillip Runkel, Susan Mountin, ed., *Dorothy Day and the Catholic Worker Movement: Centenary Essays* (Milwaukee: Marquette University Press, 2001), 169–183.

through compassionate service or civil disobedience, and often at much personal cost. Day's decision to enact God's love in the world did not simply involve addressing the world's needs through hard work—it involved an utter abandonment of the self, and a faith that by witnessing to the Truth, we participate in the redemptive acts of God. Lawrence Holben details these self-emptying aspects of Day's personalism:

> Personalism costs. It calls us to an embrace of our limitations; it invites us to stand with the weak, the poor, the anguished and the despised, not just because they need us, but because we recognize that we are already one with them. Personalism challenges us to let go of the safety nets of privilege, the protections and security we so carefully build into our lives.[11]

Nonviolence, for Day, was the active expression of self-emptying. She looked to the Sermon on the Mount for this understanding of nonviolence—a practice of loving one's enemies, doing good to those who hate you, and turning the other cheek. In Jesus' words and own life, Day witnessed the exemplar of self-emptying love. She considered love to be incompatible with violence, which in her understanding included any attempt at coercion, domination, or the manipulation of another person. Instead she believed that true love involves the laying down of one's life. Thus, as a fundamental component of nonviolence, Day's personalist approach was a spiritual expression made manifest in a response to societal injustices.[12]

Voluntary Poverty

Voluntary poverty and service to the poor served as vivid expressions of Day's embrace of personalism and nonviolence. Voluntary poverty consisted of simple sufficiency, with whatever surplus one might have belonging to others. For Day, voluntary poverty was expressed in a multitude of ways, such as stripping oneself of material wealth as both penance and an act of love, eating foods from one's own geographical region, possessing a bare minimum of clothing—clothing produced under acceptable working conditions.[13] Day's understanding of voluntary poverty also included keeping one's work honest and free from exploitation or violence:

---

11. Lawrence Holben, *All the Way to Heaven: A Theological Reflection on Dorothy Day, Peter Maurin, and the Catholic Worker* (Marion, SD: Rose Hill Books, 1997), 33.

12. Chernus, *American Nonviolence*, 154.

13. See Day, *The Long Loneliness*. See also Annice Callahan, *Spiritual Guides for Today* (New York: Crossroad, 1992), 51.

> All our talks about peace and the weapons of the spirit are meaningless unless we try in every way to embrace *voluntary poverty* and not work in any position, any job, that contributes to war, not to take any job whose pay comes from the fear of war, of the atom bomb.[14]

The self-sacrifice entailed in voluntary poverty included suffering as well. One could not only see the sight of the suffering poor, or even give all that one has in order to share with others: "One must live with them, share with them their suffering too. Give up one's privacy, and mental and spiritual comforts as well as physical."[15]

Day's emphasis on voluntary poverty was primarily directed towards those members of the population who enjoyed wealth, power, status and influence.[16] She believed that renunciation and disempowerment were fundamental to the conversion of the oppressor. Such disempowerment could be attained by adopting voluntary poverty and nonviolence as a way of life, abandoning one's security, and entering into solidarity with the powerless. By so doing, the wealthy and influential abandon themselves to divine providence and witness to God's love.

Day certainly saw practical reasons for embracing a simpler lifestyle; however, the most significant reasons for voluntary poverty ran much deeper than practicality. Such poverty not only allowed a sense of solidarity with the poor, but also permitted people to experience the shame of poverty for themselves as it ran contrary to a culture of success, power, and wealth. Perhaps most importantly, poverty resulted in what Day termed "precarity," a permanent lack of security. Precarity served to enhance the spiritual life in a number of ways. By forcing dependence on the unstable circumstances outside of one's control, precarity was a constant reminder of our complete dependence on God—a position rarely realized in a culture of entitlements, self-sufficiency and autonomy. To step outside of this mainstream culture was to see things more clearly. Wrote Day: "We cannot even see our brothers in need without first stripping ourselves."[17] For Day, this solidarity with others and dependence on God which could be

---

14. Dorothy Day, *On Pilgrimage* (New York: Catholic Worker Books, 1948), 82–83. Quoted in Callahan, *Spiritual Guides for Today*, 52.

15. Day, *The Long Loneliness*, 214.

16. Matthew R. Smith, "The Catholic Worker Movement: Toward a Theology of Liberation for First World Disciples," in William Thorn, ed., *Dorothy Day and the Catholic Worker Movement: Centenary Essays*, 161.

17. Robert Ellsberg, ed., *Dorothy Day: Selected Writings* (Maryknoll, NY: Orbis Books, 2002), 109.

realized through the precarity of voluntary poverty were inherent to a life of nonviolence.

In addition, voluntary poverty provided a detachment that liberates one from concern for the consequences of action, an important aspect of Day's personalism and a vital component of nonviolence. Through a renunciation of the fruit of action, we are able to focus on whether such actions are worthy in and of themselves and we are unlikely to compromise nonviolent means in order to attain desired ends. "Poverty is adopted gladly, because in it we discover liberation. As we let go of the comforts and protections of the bourgeois world, we find ourselves free to make personalist choices without having to calculate their potential cost."[18] Many did not understand why she chose certain actions that had no guarantee of success. She writes, for example, of a conversation with a Socialist who asserted that going to the people was a futile effort:

> I kept repeating that the Christian point of view was to keep in mind the failure of the Cross. . . . I spoke of the natural order itself, how the seed must fall into the ground and die in order to bear fruit. In the labor movement every strike is considered a failure, a loss of wages and man power, and no one is ever convinced that understanding between employer and worker is any clearer or that gains have been made on either side; and yet in the history of labor, certainly there has been a slow and steady bettering of conditions.[19]

Others also disagreed with her refusal to compromise her means for a greater effectiveness. The Association of Catholic Trade Unionists, for example, disagreed with "our loss of the opportunity to get our own men into positions of vantage in order to influence others. Maurin, however, talked about Christ's technique, of working from the bottom and with the few, of self-discipline and self-organization, of sacrifice rather than enlightened self-interest."[20] Indeed, the Catholic Worker movement tended to be non-pragmatic and oftentimes ineffectual. Rev. Roger A. Statnick writes of this significant aspect of Dorothy Day's movement:

> In this world's terms, it would look at best odd and at worst foolish when measured by concrete and lasting results. Voluntary poverty has done little to re-distribute wealth in this country. Worker pacifism during World War II decimated support for the movement and certainly did little to restrain the war effort . . . . This way is not

18. Holben, *All the Way to Heaven*, 39.
19. Day, *The Long Loneliness*, 216–17.
20. Ibid., 221.

the way of this world.... Things are measured against their source in divine creation and their destiny in the eternal Kingdom.[21]

Love, not effective results, was the measure for Day and a life of nonviolence.

Dorothy Day's commitment to service, poverty and nonviolence were not merely born from any well-defined intellectual theory or doctrinal analysis. Rather, her dedication seemed to emerge from her deepest self and her religious experience. Her love of God and love of neighbor were deeply intertwined in her spiritual practice. The suffering and sacrifice of her day-to-day service were aimed just as much at union with Christ as were her spiritual retreats that helped her to "put on the mind of Christ" and prepared her for her difficult work. Fed by the spiritual renewal received from one of her frequent retreats, Day noted that "Every action must receive [the] touch of Christ.... The only way is to do it *for Christ*. Not for self. The only thing which gives importance to actions is Christ."[22] The love, detachment, and suffering that were such profound elements of her life of service, were at the same time fundamental elements of her dedication to Christ.

Day and Douglass

It was Day's heart-centered dedication and sacrifice that profoundly impacted Douglass. Day served to exemplify not how nonviolence is best theorized but how it is lived out in one's life. Her exemplary role in Douglass's life began early on, when he was an undergraduate student at Santa Clara University. In his book, *The Nonviolent Coming of God*, James Douglass details how he first learned of Dorothy Day. The year was 1957, and Douglass was a student of Herbert Burke, an English professor at the university. Burke had given the students an article describing Dorothy Day and other Catholic Workers' non-cooperation during the civil defense drills. Douglass recalls that upon reading the article, the students

---

21. Roger A. Statnick, "Dorothy Day: Citizen of the Kingdom," in William Thorn, ed., *Dorothy Day and the Catholic Worker Movement: Centenary Essays*, 377.

22. Dorothy Day, "All is Grace" Manuscript, Marquette University Archives, 173–74. Quoted in Brigid O'Shea Merriman, *Searching for Christ: The Spirituality of Dorothy Day* (Notre Dame, IN: University of Notre Dame Press, 1994), 149. See Merriman's work for an in-depth analysis of Day's spirituality and its relationship to her commitment to social justice and the marginalized. Merriman's attention to Day's retreats reveals the extent to which these events informed Day's quest for ascetical perfection and critique of bourgeois Christianity.

determined that Day was crazy. The story of Day however had a profound influence on Douglass:

> Looking back now, three decades later, I remember that spring at Santa Clara as one long meditation on Dorothy Day, her friends in the park, and the world's threatened destruction by nuclear war.... I discovered that resisting nuclear war preparations was for the Catholic Worker movement all of a piece with feeding the hungry, sheltering the homeless, and resisting every kind of injustice. All of it was building a new society, the kingdom of God, within the shell of the old. Jesus' vision of God's kingdom is why Dorothy Day had gone to the park and to jail.[23]

In an article published in *Katallagete*, Douglass further describes that early influence of Day and The Catholic Worker:

> That first encounter with Dorothy Day and the Catholic Worker put me in living contact with a tradition whose richness has deepened for me over the years—the tradition of faith and suffering love, at the center of the Church and extending through the centuries of martyrs ("witnesses") to the cross of Christ. As I began reading *The Catholic Worker*, I recognized a community living out the Gospel, whose professions of non-violence represented the life of Christ in the America of the '50's: a life of voluntary poverty in service to the involuntarily destitute, a life of following Providence, of practicing the works of mercy, of resisting a warfare state with non-violent civil disobedience; a life and way corresponding to Jesus' cross. My introduction to non-violence, through the Catholic Worker, was therefore an experience embodied in a community of faith, with the global context of an impending nuclear end of time.[24]

Douglass received the privilege of meeting Day while still a student at Santa Clara. Over dinner with a number of other students, "I divulged that I was in the Army Reserve and Dorothy immediately snapped, 'How long are you going to continue to do that?' And she gave me a very level look across the table and I became extremely uncomfortable."[25] With that one level look, Dorothy Day would challenge Douglass for the rest of his life—calling him to reflect on his own conscience, integrity, and wholeness of self. Through that look and the example she led, Day converted Douglass to her vision for the world. Douglass referred to her later as the

---

23. Douglass, *The Nonviolent Coming of God*, 99.
24. James Douglass, "Non-Violence and Metanoia," 26.
25. As cited in Preston, "Seeking the Reign of God," 24.

"leaven" that transformed his life, "a holy burr in my conscience, prickly but saintly."[26]

Douglass encountered Day again while lobbying the bishops at Vatican II. He was particularly impressed by the women's ten-day fast led by Day in Rome in 1965. "The women's fast, and Dorothy Day's in particular, went to the heart of the total war question: the hunger of the world's destitute beneath the waste and terror of the arms race." For Douglass, the fast was "the most profoundly transforming leaven of the final session of the Vatican Council" and personally inspirational.[27] Nearly three decades later, Douglass, with his wife Shelley, would move to Birmingham to open a Catholic Worker House.

Mahatma Gandhi

As significant members of the American Peace Movement, both Dorothy Day and James Douglass were strongly influenced by the nonviolence of Gandhi. Both Gandhi's experience with a nonviolent lifestyle and his intellectual philosophy of nonviolence find prominence throughout Douglass's works. Indeed, Gandhi's presence is second only to Jesus in Douglass's writings. He served as a near-contemporary whose theoretical and practical import for Douglass's theory of nonviolence cannot be overestimated.

Mohandas Gandhi was born in 1869 in the state of Gujarat in India to a middle-class, orthodox Vaishnavite family. Of his youth and religious education he stated, "One thing took deep root in me—the conviction that morality is the basis of things, and that truth is the substance of all morality. Truth became my sole objective. It began to grow in magnitude every day, and my definition of it also has been ever widening."[28] At the age of eighteen, he pursued a law degree in London, passing the bar in 1891. Two years later, Gandhi moved to South Africa, where he stayed for two decades practicing law and working for Indian rights. It was here that he formulated his philosophies of life and of *Satyagraha*, or 'truth-force,' as well as resisting injustice and correcting systemic wrongs. After leading Indians to defy oppressive South African law, serving time in prison, and conducting the first of many political fasts, he returned to India in 1914 with his ideas on nonviolence.[29]

26. Douglass, *The Nonviolent Coming of God*, 99.
27. Ibid., 101–2.
28. J. B. Kripalani, *Gandhi: His Life and Thought* (Delhi: Publications Division, Ministry of Information and Broadcasting, Government of India, 1971), 4.
29. For a helpful exploration of Gandhi's life, see Stanley A. Wolpert, *Gandhi's Passion:*

The Community of Influence

Sixteen years later, Gandhi began his campaign of civil disobedience to free India from the colonial oppression of the British. The Salt March to the Sea was one such action of disobedience that had a profound impact on both Gandhi's movement and proponents of nonviolence in the West. In 1930, Gandhi walked 241 kilometers to the Arabian Sea to make his own salt, thereby violating the laws that guarded Britain's salt monopoly in India. Gandhi's gesture spurred millions of Indians to defy the salt laws by making their own salt. As a result, the British were overwhelmed with the magnitude of required arrests and although they themselves employed violent tactics to coerce submission from the resisters, the Indians remained completely nonviolent. Despite the fact that it would take seventeen more years for India to become officially independent, the Salt March won for many Indians the freedom to resist British law and a recognition of their own nonviolent power. Because it called for the personal sacrifice of millions, the Salt March also revealed the potential for effective nonviolence on a massive scale. James Douglass was particularly impressed with the spirit of the march and the momentum it created. In *Resistance and Contemplation* he writes, "In terms of human consciousness, Gandhi's march may have been the most important political event to have taken place since Jesus' execution by the Romans. . . ."[30]

Gandhi continued his leadership of the *swaraj*, or liberation movement, alternating periods of fasting, boycotting, and prison terms. He also worked on behalf of the untouchables, improving their treatment by the British government. A year after India gained its independence from British Rule in 1947, Gandhi was shot and killed by a Hindu traditionalist.

This life of spiritual practices and lived resistance to injustice strongly impacted Douglass's understanding of nonviolence as actively undertaken "experiments in Truth." Yet equally influential were Gandhi's ideas concerning nonviolence, ideas deeply rooted in his religion and spirituality. We will briefly consider Gandhi's religious beliefs in order to better explore his understanding of nonviolence with its themes of Truth, sacrifice, and freedom.

Gandhi's religion was a mélange of both modern and traditional Hinduism, influenced by Western thought and other religious traditions. He was receptive to influences such as Jainism and Buddhism, for example, and his three years in London developed his interest in Christianity, particularly in the figure of Jesus and the New Testament. Consequently, he did not feel compelled to adhere to all of Hindu tradition. One can certainly hear the Upanishads in Gandhi's understanding of Brahman as the

The Life and Legacy of Mahatma Gandhi (New York: Oxford University Press, 2001).
30. James Douglass, *Resistance and Contemplation: The Way of Liberation*, 85.

essence of all that is—the abiding, immutable, and fundamental reality. Yet because of his receptivity to Western ideas, Gandhi was able to equate God with Brahman. He widened the definition even further to see Brahman, or God, as "the pattern of relationships among all things, the way that all realities are bound together and interact as parts of the single ultimate reality."[31] For Gandhi, God was Reality, or *sat* in Sanskrit—the Life Force of endless change, simultaneously immanent and transcendent.

Truth

Significant to Gandhi's understanding of nonviolence was the correlation of *sat*, the utterly real, with Truth. "The word *satya* [truth] is derived from *sat*, which means that which is. *Satya* means a state of being. Nothing is or exists in reality except Truth. That is why *sat* or *satya* is the right name for God."[32] Gandhi moved from conceiving of God as Truth to asserting, rather, that Truth is God. For Gandhi, Truth is the only reason for our existence and as a result, our lives should concentrate upon it. "Truth," wrote Gandhi, "should be the very breath of our life. . . ."[33] Gandhian religion becomes therefore the lifelong quest for Truth, and in the attainment of this Truth, the soul's perfection. When one reaches pure Truth, one's essential self transcends the ego, becoming identical with Brahman. In this state, one participates in Truth through one's knowledge, thoughts, and deeds.[34]

If Truth is the goal of life, then, for Gandhi, desire is that which keeps us from attaining it. Desire encourages the ego and intensifies the illusory sense of separation from others. To extinguish desire is to extinguish the ego, and one "who has achieved extinction of the ego becomes the very image of Truth."[35] One of the most significant ways of transcending the ego is overcoming self-love by loving others, a requirement for reaching God. Incompatible with self-interest, love requires that we reduce ourselves to nothing—that we serve others through selflessness. For Gandhi, selfless service was the key to life and Truth. Believing that survival depended upon the sacrifices of others, Gandhi's call to service necessitated sacrifice and mutual giving.

31. Chernus, *American Nonviolence*, 94.
32. Raghavan Iyer, ed., *The Essential Writings of Mahatma Gandhi* (New Delhi: Oxford University Press, 2004), 231.
33. Ibid., 233.
34. Chernus, *American Nonviolence*, 94–95.
35. Iyer, ed., *The Essential Writings of Mahatma Gandhi*, 227.

> Loving dutiful sacrifice is the eternally true pattern. . . . Any act that helps keep the pattern going is participation in Truth and brings the doer closer to Truth. Therefore, serving others is not serving discrete individual things. It is serving *sat*, ultimate reality itself. Any act that aims to serve *sat* is a manifestation of *sat*. It is *satya*, a true act, an act of Truth.[36]

Sacrificial service was therefore not simply valuable for its attained ends, but was itself a manifestation of the Truth, Reality, and God. Gandhi's understanding of loving service also necessitated overcoming one's fear, as fear is incompatible with love. When we empty ourselves, we have nothing to lose and nothing to fear, and are therefore fully able to abandon ourselves to love and Truth.

The notion of Truth, with its elements of service and fearlessness, is vital to Gandhi's concept of nonviolence. Because the quest for Truth was at the center of his understanding of religion, Gandhi's emphasis on nonviolence was grounded in this search for Truth. According to Gandhi, violence, or *himsa*, involves coercing another person to comply with one's own selfish desire. It is therefore born out of an attachment to the ego and is incompatible with seeking the Truth. By concentrating on one's own desire, one is blind to the truth that every person's well-being is tied up with one another and that all are connected in the same Reality. Nonviolence, or *ahimsa*, on the other hand, fundamentally involves adherence to Truth. Rather than placing the focus on victory or even self-preservation, nonviolence prioritizes Truth. The opponent then becomes secondary to the real challenge—maintaining one's commitment to Truth. As no one can lay claim to Absolute Truth, however, one must be open to finding it in new places. Knowledge of the Truth is risky. If we think we know, Truth then asks us to act, to experiment, to lay ourselves bare to its demands. Hence, Gandhi entitled his autobiography *The Story of My Experiments with Truth*, as it spoke of a lifetime of Gandhi's own practice of and search for Truth.

Sacrifice, Suffering, and the Rejection of Consequences

Sacrifice and suffering were inherent to Gandhi's theory of nonviolence. Instead of a passivism that capitulates to the powerful to protect the self, *ahimsa* resists untruth even at the expense of one's life. Nonviolence is thus incompatible with self-interest—only one who lacks ego-attachment can both know the Truth and stand up for it. As Gandhi writes, "the quest of Truth involves *tapascharya*, self-suffering, sometimes unto death. There

---

36. Chernus, *American Nonviolence*, 98.

can be no place in it for even a trace of self-interest."[37] Yet not only does nonviolence forbid self-interest, it also demands sacrifice and suffering. Nonviolence involves not merely the absence of violence, but acting with selfless love and sacrificial service for others. The willingness to suffer is an important element of such loving *ahimsa*. A willing acceptance of suffering helps to purify people of attachments to fear and ego while, conversely, the less attachments one clings to, the more suffering one can endure. A willingness to endure suffering opens one up to the Truth because it diminishes the obstructions created by self-interest. This can be witnessed in acts of nonviolence where one chooses to accept suffering or wrongdoing in order to maintain principles of Truth rather than inflict suffering on others for the sake of the ego. In order to practice this manner of nonviolence one must not be restricted by fear. "Those alone can follow the path of nonviolent resistance," writes Gandhi, "who are free from fear, whether as to their possessions, false honor, their relatives, the government, bodily injuries or death."[38] Inasmuch as it demands knowledge of and adherence to Truth, sacrifice, and fearlessness, nonviolence is not as much a moral code as an awareness of and participation in Reality, or God.

Through this participation in Reality, actions based on Truth are the central concern of the nonviolent person, not the consequences of them. Nonviolence involves both the way one acts as well as the goal toward which one moves. "Nonviolence is the law of life for human beings. For me it is both a means and an end."[39] Living from a place of selfless love by adhering to Truth is the sole focus of a nonviolent life. If the means by which one lives are nonviolent, then the consequences will bear the stamp of Truth and love. "The means," wrote Gandhi, "may be likened to a seed, the end to a tree; and there is just the same inviolable connection between the means and the end as there is between the seed and the tree."[40] If one employs means other than an adherence to Truth, the results will naturally be tainted with untruth: one cannot expect to use violence to obtain peace. Thus one should focus primarily on how one behaves rather than the outcome of the acts. Conduct, not results, is what brings us closer to the Truth. For Gandhi, a detachment from consequences was vital to nonviolence. One cannot be concerned with effective results or one will likely compromise the nonviolent means.

37. Iyer, ed., *The Essential Writings of Mahatma Gandhi*, 233.
38. Dennis Dalton, ed., *Mahatma Gandhi: Selected Political Writings* (Indianapolis: Hackett Publishing Company, Inc., 1996), 13.
39. Iyer, ed., *The Essential Writings of Mahatma Gandhi*, 244.
40. M. K. Gandhi, *Non-Violent Resistance* (New York: Schocken Books, 1961), 10.

Freedom

Through this desire-less nonviolence, one experiences true freedom, or *swaraj*. Political freedom was certainly a significant component of *swaraj*, as witnessed in Gandhi's work for Indian independence, Indian rights in South Africa, and the rights of the untouchables. In the service of Truth, one must inevitably work for the freedom of persons, individually and collectively. For Gandhi, however, *swaraj* was primarily religious. "I am not interested in freeing India merely from the English yoke," he wrote. "I am bent upon freeing India from any yoke whatsoever."[41] Gandhi believed that the heaviest yoke was that of desire; therefore, real freedom involved purification from the desire generated by ego-attachment. Freedom from such desire permits one to act nonviolently; that is, to act lovingly and truthfully even if it entails suffering or negative consequences.

Gandhi's nonviolent political actions were therefore also fundamentally religious ones: He worked from his own internal freedom to bring others to *swaraj* as well, believing that only then would political freedom follow. Those who are inwardly free, after all, may not be coerced: "The outward freedom therefore that we shall attain will only be in exact proportion to the inward freedom to which we may have grown at any given moment. And if this is the correct view of freedom, our chief energy must be concentrated upon reform from within."[42] Only inward freedom gives a person the external freedoms of self-rule and self-control. Indeed, because no one can force inwardly free persons to commit unwilled acts, the real power resides in those with inner freedom, even if they appear externally powerless through imprisonment or oppression. According to Gandhi, the Indian *swaraj* required this freedom. "[Gandhi] said that the Indians were enslaved to the British only because they let themselves be. On the day that they chose to embrace nonviolence, rise above their fear, and refuse to follow the British rules and rulers, they would begin to act like free people."[43] Although it would take time, political freedom would be an inevitable consequence. "Imagine a whole people," wrote Gandhi, "unwilling to conform to the laws of the legislature, and prepared to suffer the consequences of non-compliance. They will bring the whole legislature and executive machinery to a

---

41. Dalton, ed., *Mahatma Gandhi: Selected Political Writings*, 120.

42. Mahatma Gandhi, *The Collective Works of Mahatma Gandhi*, vol. 38 (Delhi: Publications Division, Ministry of Information and Broadcasting, Government of India, 1958–94), 1–2. Quoted in Dalton, ed., *Mahatma Gandhi: Selected Political Writings*, 97–98.

43. Chernus, *American Nonviolence*, 106.

standstill."[44] Thus political freedom necessarily begins with internal freedom; that is, adherence to the Truth through nonviolence.

Satyagraha: Gandhian Nonviolence

Gandhi coined the term *Satyagraha* to mean the active resistance that embodies the adherence to Truth, fearless service, sacrifice, and freedom of nonviolence. Gandhi articulated its origin and meaning in a Statement to the Hunter Committee:

> The term *Satyagraha* was coined by me in South Africa to express the force that the Indians there used for full eight years and it was coined in order to distinguish it from the movement then going on in the United Kingdom and South Africa under the name of Passive Resistance. Its root meaning is holding on to truth, hence truth-force. I have also called it Love-force or Soul-force. In the application of Satyagraha I discovered in the earliest stages that pursuit of truth did not admit violence being inflicted on one's opponent but that he must be weaned from error by patience and sympathy. For what appears to be truth to the one may appear to be error to the other. And patience means self-suffering. So the doctrine came to mean vindication of truth not by infliction of suffering on the opponent but on one's self.[45]

Satyagraha, for Gandhi, was extremely gentle. It could not stem from anger or malice, and could never wound nor even wish evil upon another. A Satyagrahi, or practitioner of *Satyagraha*, adhered to the Truth, regardless of consequences. Thus, Satyagrahis were known to endure beatings and death in their persistent refusal to back down in the face of injustice. As a result, *Satyagraha* came to imply civil disobedience for many. Yet it maintained its roots in the deep religiousness of Gandhi, and the spiritual basis of his nonviolent ideals.

Gandhi and Douglass

Douglass first encountered Gandhi's ideas of *Satyagraha* while a student at Santa Clara University. In the decades following, Douglass found Gandhi's development of nonviolence increasingly important for his own theology and practice of nonviolence. *Satyagraha* provided Douglass with both a practical example of lived nonviolent resistance as well as a successful integration of spirituality with political and social justice. Gandhi was, for

---

44. Dalton, ed., *Mahatma Gandhi: Selected Political Writings*, 107.
45. Gandhi, *Non-Violent Resistance*, 6.

Douglass, an example of the possible. More than that, Gandhi was a figure not unlike Christ. Douglass describes Gandhi's measure of influence in *The Nonviolent Cross:*

> In the modern world the meeting of man and God has most closely approximated the revolution of the cross in the person of Mohandas Gandhi. While it cannot be said that to preach Gandhism is to preach Christ, it is always necessary to preach Christ in terms of his continuing presence in man and of the upward revolution of cross and open tomb; their primary exponent in our time is Gandhi. The significance of Gandhi is that more than any other man of our century, except Pope John XXIII on a different level of politics, he has testified to the active presence of God in the world of political man and has done so after the pattern of Jesus. In Gandhi belief met secularity in suffering love and an empire changed.[46]

For Douglass, Gandhi served as an accessible, contemporary exemplar of the Reality of God breaking into history through nonviolence. As Douglass writes in *Lightning East to West*, "The revolutionary truth of Gandhi lies in what he became through his experiments, an objective force of truth and love, what Gandhi called 'a satyagrahi'."[47] Gandhian nonviolence buttressed Douglass's own deeply-held belief that nonviolence is more than a passive refusal to do harm, or even an active confrontation with violence. Both men asserted that nonviolence bears an intrinsic connection to God and serves to empty the ego in order to welcome the objective Reality of Truth and of God.

In *The Nonviolent Cross*, Douglass writes of Gandhi as a remarkable exemplar of political and spiritual convergence:

> Gandhi's faith and politics were inseparable. . . . Gandhi rejected the popular description of himself as a saint trying to be a politician; he said that the truth was the other way around. Yet the extent to which Gandhi as a politician made his goal, that of seeing God face to face, determine and form each of his concrete actions and policies sets him far apart from any other believing politician. He made God his end not as a terminal point and his particular salvation but as the Reality to be progressively found through his daily politics, the ground and measure of every decision, and as an end already visible in the faces of a people resisting oppression with love. Gandhi was

---

46 Douglass, *The Non-Violent Cross*, 33.
47. Douglass, *Lightning East to West*, 21.

both saint and politician because his deepening vision of God was realized in and through his political vision for man.[48]

Like Gandhi, Douglass sought to make his own life's work center on the search for spiritual truth, of which political involvement was derivative. He therefore explored the many facets of Gandhian nonviolence and considered them through a Catholic frame of reference. As we will see in the following chapters, a great deal of Douglass's own nonviolent theory reflects the main themes of Gandhian nonviolence, including an acceptance of suffering, liberation from the ego, detachment from the fruit of one's actions, and an adherence to Truth, or God.

Gandhi had a tremendous influence on the theory and practice of nonviolence in the United States. James Douglass and Dorothy Day were two such persons profoundly influenced by Gandhi's thought. Thomas Merton was another who found that Gandhi's nonviolent ideals resonated deeply with his own Christian position on peace and social justice. Merton intermingled Gandhi's theories on *Satyagraha* with his own contemplative bent to produce a view of Christian nonviolence that was at once deeply spiritual and intensely involved in the world. Like Gandhi, Merton's ideas also had a significant impact on Douglass's thought and so it is to his intellectual influence that we now turn.

Thomas Merton

Thomas Merton was born in France in 1915. For the first twenty-three years of his life he lived what he called "rank savage paganism" until his conversion to Catholicism in 1938.[49] Feeling called to enter the priesthood, in 1942 he applied to the Trappist Abbey of Gethsemani in Kentucky. He remained in this contemplative order until his death in 1968. Educated in the English language and a gifted writer, Merton is best known for his numerous spiritual writings, journals, and letters. His involvement in the Catholic peace community and his concern for social justice, however, were also vital components of his life. His writings on the subject contributed significantly to the peace movements of the 1960s and beyond.

---

48. Douglass, *The Non-Violent Cross*, 34.

49. Thomas Merton, *The Seven Storey Mountain*, 50th anniversary ed. (New York: Harcourt Brace, 1998), 237. *The Seven Storey Mountain* is Merton's autobiography about his early life and the years immediately following his conversion. For additional biographical information, see Michael Mott, *The Seven Mountains of Thomas Merton* (Boston: Houghton Mifflin, 1984).

Merton divided his writings into three periods. The first period, between 1938 and 1949, was primarily ascetic and apocalyptic. These writings revealed his newness to the Christian faith and an uncritical acceptance of the popular separation between God and the world. In the second period between 1949 and 1959, Merton moved to incorporate incarnational thought more fully. During his third period from 1959 onward, Merton self-consciously tried to integrate God and the world while focusing on the social issues of his day. He no longer viewed contemplation as a means of withdrawing from the world, but rather as a way to be better involved in it. His attention to poverty and race, along with the Cold War and Christian-Marxist dialogue led to numerous discourses on peace. Because of Merton's giftedness with prose, his reputation as a conventional spiritual writer, and the credence that accompanies a monastic life, he held a much wider audience than did others from the Catholic Left. His ideas on nonviolence, politics, and justice, as well as those on contemplation and theological matters had an important influence on many both within and outside of the Catholic peace community.[50]

Within the peace movement, Merton contributed in a number of ways. First, he articulated a shift that was occurring in the 1950's as the movement moved intellectually from rationales based on the just war theory and pacifism to those centered on nonviolent resistance. Second, Merton communicated the relevance of Gandhian nonviolence to the Christian faith. Third, and most important to our purposes here, Merton eloquently articulated the intrinsic connection between personal spirituality and social involvement. As all three of these contributions served to develop Douglass's own nonviolent theology, it is worth exploring each in greater depth.

From the Just War to Nonviolence

One of Merton's contributions to the peace movement was an articulation of the changing approaches to peace taking place in the middle of the century.[51] Like activists the world over, Merton believed that the tensions of the Cold War—conceived in ideology and incarnated militarily—severely threatened the globe and portended a possible nuclear holocaust. Merton determined that Christian ethics had been warped by the sever-

---

50. McNeal, *The American Catholic Peace Movement*, 128–30.

51. For an excellent compilation of Merton's writings on peace, see Thomas Merton, *The Nonviolent Alternative*, ed. Gordon C. Zahn (New York: Farrar, Straus, and Giroux, 1980).

ity of this Cold War threat. Although he adhered initially to the logic of the traditional just war theory, Merton later found this theory irrelevant in the modern situation where nuclear weapons threatened millions of noncombatants and radically altered the face of war. He concluded that the just war rationale was inadequate when confronted by the reality of nuclear weapons: "A war of total annihilation simply cannot be considered a 'Just War' no matter how good the causes for which it is undertaken."[52] Merton was not, however, a complete pacifist and did not totally reject the just war theory. Because he could not concede that a war could never be just, he qualified his position by referring to himself as a nuclear pacifist. With the Vietnam War, however, Merton began to question whether even limited wars could ever be just. His previous distinctions between limited and nuclear wars gradually faded in his later writings as he sought a new peace ethic apart from the just war ethic.[53]

Much like his position on the Just War, Merton considered pacifism to be problematic in the face of nuclear weapons. He disputed pacifism on a number of grounds. First, he disagreed with any rationale that relied on individual conscience rather than social direction. In addition, he found the term religiously ambiguous—it did not have the same connotation as 'peacemakers,' which was the true work of Jesus' followers.[54] Finally, Merton had difficulty condemning the violence of the oppressed: "If the oppressed try to resist by force—which is their right—theology has no business preaching non-violence to them. Mere blind destruction is, of course, futile and immoral: but who are we to condemn a desperation we have helped to cause!"[55]

Like many in the American peace movement, Merton turned to a theology of nonviolence in an effort to move beyond the inadequacies of pacifism and the just war ethic. He embraced nonviolence for its ability to speak to the spiritual problem of violence as it relates to both individuals and society. Nonviolence, he wrote, "is not built on a presupposed division, but on the basic unity of man. It is not out for the conversion of the wicked to the

---

52. Thomas P. McDonnell, ed., *A Thomas Merton Reader* (New York: 1962), 291. Quoted in McNeal, *The American Catholic Peace Movement*, 136.

53. McNeal, *The American Catholic Peace Movement*, 136. See also David W. Givey, *The Social Thought of Thomas Merton: The Way of Nonviolence and Peace for the Future* (Chicago: Franciscan Herald Press, 1983), 50–57.

54. McNeal, *The American Catholic Peace Movement*, 139–41. See also Givey, *The Social Thought of Thomas Merton*, 57–60.

55. Thomas Merton, *Faith and Violence: Christian Teaching and Christian Practice* (Notre Dame, IN: University of Notre Dame Press, 1994), 8.

ideas of the good, but for the healing and reconciliation of man with himself, man the person and man the human family."[56] Unlike the just war doctrine and pacifism, nonviolence for Merton was an exacting form of struggle that "excludes mere transient self-interest from its considerations."[57]

Merton's call for nonviolent resistance was strengthened by his scathing critiques of structural injustice as supported by the Church and reinforced by the media, technology, and the American religion of capitalism. He considered America a sick nation fed by the illusions that force is necessary and that power is central to human relationships. "Violence today," he wrote, "is white-collar violence, the systematically organized bureaucratic and technological destruction of man."[58] Pacifism and the just war theory could not respond to such violence. Nonviolent resistance, however, as the living of the Kingdom, confronted even deeply embedded structural violence.

Merton and Gandhi

Much of Merton's thought was fed by his reading of Gandhian nonviolence. His concise interpretation of Gandhi's thought was as follows:

> [Gandhi's] way was no secret: it was simply to follow conscience without regard for the consequences to himself, in the belief that this was demanded of him by God and that the results would be the work of God. Perhaps indeed for a long time these results would remain hidden as God's secret. But in the end the truth would manifest itself.[59]

Merton found Gandhian nonviolence compatible with the Christian faith for two main reasons. Both Gandhian nonviolence and the Gospel valued a willing acceptance of suffering in order to avoid inflicting suffering on others. In addition, both held that truth should be the means as well as the end of one's striving. Holding to truth as both the way and the goal, they rendered insignificant any worldly consideration of effectiveness.

After absorbing much of Gandhi's view on nonviolence as it relates to truth and spirituality, Merton added an eschatological dimension to make it compatible with the Christian tradition. Believing that nonviolence be-

---

56. Merton, *The Nonviolent Alternative*, 209.

57. Ibid., 208.

58. Merton, *Faith and Violence*, 6. For Merton's condensed views on Gandhi, see his work entitled "A Tribute to Gandhi" in Merton, *The Nonviolent Alternative*, 178–84.

59. Thomas Merton, *Seeds of Destruction* (New York: Farrar, Straus, and Giroux, 1964), 225.

longed to God's Kingdom, Merton asserted that Christ's Second Coming is necessarily intrinsic to the victory of truth that Gandhi sought. He held that a reign of peace and justice could only coincide with the Second Coming, which requires first a conversion to love. "Christian peace," wrote Merton, "was an eschatological gift of the Risen Christ. (John 20:19) It could not be achieved by any ethical or political program. . . . Christian peace is in fact a fruit of the Spirit (Galatians 5:22) and a sign of the Divine Presence in the world."[60] Holding the 'long view' that a new heaven and earth would be created with the Second Coming of Christ, Merton believed that in the meantime, the Church would be in a constant struggle with worldly powers, with war clearly belonging to the world and not to the Kingdom. Optimistic about the human contribution to the Kingdom, Merton understood that Christ would come through the human embrace of truth and love and through the spiritual discovery of a fuller humanity. Nonviolence, for Merton, was this living of the Kingdom. Drawing from Gandhi, Merton's nonviolence involved an inner transformation whereby one could suffer for truth and share Christ's selfless love rather than inflicting violence out of self-interest and fear.

This integration of Gandhian nonviolence with Christianity was one of Merton's great contributions to the Catholic peace movement. He articulated the relevance of Gandhi to the West in *Seeds of Destruction*:

> What is certainly true is that Gandhi not only understood the ethic of the Gospel as well, if not in some ways better, than many Christians, but he is one of the very few men of our time who applied Gospel principles to the problems of a political and social existence in such a way that his approach to these problems was *inseparably* religious and political at the same time.[61]

In Gandhi, Merton witnessed a rare vision of political and religious integration, one he himself knew as inherent to Christianity but only rarely acknowledged. Let us further examine how Merton explicated this integrated view of nonviolence for the Christian peace movement.

The Connection between Spirituality and Social Change

Like Gandhi, Merton understood the quest for justice and peace to be rooted in spirituality. As a prolific writer on the spiritual life and contemplation, Merton expressed well the fundamental role of spiritual-

---

60. Ibid., 127.
61. Ibid., 226.

ity in Christian nonviolence, an idea that was exceedingly important for Douglass. For Merton, personal transformation and social change were inextricably linked, and conversion was necessary to a changed social order. While many in the peace movement looked to revolution to usher in a reign of justice and peace, Merton looked to the presence of Christ made manifest in and through spiritual transformation.

A contemplative posture is absolutely necessary, said Merton, for the ability to act nonviolently and endure suffering. In the post-Christian world of nuclear weapons and the capacity of nations for total self-destruction, Merton believed that humans were being forced to confront their spiritual selves. The sheer horror of potential apocalyptic destruction reveals our societal insanity, our efforts to construct and preserve an illusorily powerful self that is able to disregard both God and neighbor. Thus Merton saw efforts such as militarization and systematic economic exploitation as symptoms of a deeper illness still: the fortification of a false identity which protects a hidden emptiness. Similarly, Merton saw the false self behind so much of the apparently more noble but still frantic activism for peace, justice, and the transformation of political and social structures. Although these latter efforts may be good in themselves, nevertheless they too can become a means of grasping at control, relevance, and security in order not to face the poverty within. But this estrangement from "the inner ground of meaning and love" only deepens the crisis in which humankind finds itself. As Merton writes:

> He who attempts to act and do things for others or for the world without deepening his own self-understanding, freedom, integrity and capacity to love will not have anything to give others. He will communicate to them nothing but the contagion of his own obsessions, his aggressiveness, his ego-centered ambitions, his delusions about ends and means, his doctrinaire prejudices and ideas.[62]

Only in the self-transcendence of contemplation—that is, in the transformative release from the egoistic need to calculate and control—can one see the world for what it is through the eyes of God. It is therefore only in contemplation that one finds the love and strength to embrace nonviolent resistance as an entirely new way of life.[63]

---

62. Thomas Merton, *Contemplation in a World of Action* (Notre Dame, IN: University of Notre Dame Press, 1998), 160–161.

63. This relationship between spirituality and social change is seen most prominently in Merton's writing from 1959 to his death in 1968, a period during which he wrote extensively on contemplation. See works such as *New Seeds of Contemplation* (1962), *Seeds of Destruction* (1964), and *Faith and Violence* (1968).

Merton and Douglass

Merton's contributions to the Catholic peace movement were of course profoundly felt by Douglass. Douglass first encountered Merton's treatment of nuclear war in the pages of *The Catholic Worker* in 1961—the poem "Chant to Be Used in Processions around a Site with Furnaces"—which resonated with Douglass's own interest in the nuclear issue. In the decades following, Merton's writings would continue to have a strong influence on Douglass's thought. In the progression of Douglass's writings, the shift from a concern with the just war theory to a greater focus on nonviolence is akin to a similar shift in Merton's works. Additionally, one finds in Douglass a critique of technology, power structures, and Church/State embeddedness—prominent themes throughout Merton's later writings.

One also finds in Douglass the influence of Merton's Christian application of Gandhian nonviolence. "Tom Merton," wrote Douglass, "in his intense essays of war, peace, and non-violence which followed the appearance of his 'Chant,' showed the contemplative dimension of non-violence, that dimension of inner unity which made deep sense of the fact that a Hindu, Gandhi, could be the greatest modern example of the way of Christ, the way of suffering love to the point of death and transformation."[64] Thanks in part to Merton's interpretation of Gandhian nonviolence, Douglass would continue throughout his writings to expound on the Christian application of Gandhi's thought and "Experiments with Truth."

Merton's influence can perhaps be seen most lucidly in Douglass's frequent references to the significance of contemplation for nonviolence. For example, in an article entitled "Non-violence and Metanoia," Douglass establishes this connection between contemplation and nonviolence by relying on Merton:

> Non-violence in deed, said Merton, was nothing more than a living out of a non-violence of the heart, an inner unity already experienced in prayer. . . . Tom Merton's contemplative life and writings gradually revealed to me the most radical dimension of non-violence, that inner unity in silent prayer without which non-violent tactics were liable to descend from truth-force to *duragraha* (a biased, manipulative strategy), as happened increasingly in the civil rights, peace, and campus demonstrations of the 60s, from there to drain away finally in sporadic violence and mass apathy.[65]

---

64. Douglass, "Non-Violence and Metanoia," 27.
65. Ibid.

Again, Douglass writes, "The power of contemplation in the world is what one learns from Merton, almost unwillingly."[66]

For both men, contemplative spirituality was necessary for the self-emptying, or kenosis, of true nonviolence.[67] Contemplation was necessary to perceive reality from outside of the false self, the frail, evanescent mask of the 'I,' and to undergo personal transformation as a result. Indeed, both Douglass and Merton held conversion as indispensable to nonviolence. On this subject, Douglass was perhaps most impressed with Merton's last works as influenced by his encounters with Eastern religions. These works of Merton's, such as *Mystics and Zen Masters* (1967) and *Zen and the Birds of Appetite* (1968), explore the Buddhist ideas of the emptied self, liberated from the will and ego-attachment. Douglass, like Merton, found that the Zen idea of *satori*, or awakening, helped one understand Christian *metanoia*, or conversion.[68]

The conclusion to *Mystics and Zen Masters* provided Douglass with particular insight into his own work with nonviolent theology. Wrote Merton, "Is there not an 'optical illusion' in an eschatological spirit which, however much it may appeal to *agape*, seeks only to transform persons and social structures *from the outside*? Here we arrive at a basic principle, one might almost say an ontology of nonviolence, which requires further investigation."[69] Douglass responded to Merton's insight by speculating that perhaps Merton was himself investigating an ontology of nonviolence when he died. He continues: "Can we now join in such an investigation ourselves? What was Merton pointing to as that basic principle, or ontology of nonviolence, which would go beyond a 'transformation from the outside'. . . ?" As I will try to show in the following chapters, exploring an ontology of nonviolence was Douglass's life project, both intellectually and experientially. Merton was able to provide the tools for the project, including an articulation of the question.

66. Douglass, *The Non-Violent Cross*, viii.

67. Self-emptying here refers to the stripping of the "false self," which is, in essence, "our separate, external, egotistic will" that focuses in on itself and alienates us from God. See Thomas Merton, *New Seeds of Contemplation* (New York: New Directions, 1972), 21. The idea of self-emptying will be explored in subsequent chapters, as it becomes central to Douglass's understanding of the cross, and therefore, nonviolence.

68. See especially Douglass, *Resistance and Contemplation: The Way of Liberation*, 60–62.

69. Thomas Merton, *Mystics and Zen Masters* (New York: Farrar, Straus, & Giroux, 1967), 287–88. Quoted in James Douglass, "Thomas Merton's Glimpse of the Kingdom," in *The Message of Thomas Merton*, ed. Patrick Hart, *Cistercian Studies Series* (Kalamazoo: Cistercian Publications, 1981), 205.

Merton's influence on Douglass was not merely intellectual, however. Douglass had met Merton in 1965 while teaching at Bellarmine College in Kentucky. He quickly developed a personal friendship with Merton and continued to visit and correspond with him until Merton's death in 1968. Through such correspondence, Douglass shared with Merton his idea for a book, which would later become *The Nonviolent Cross*, and received advice and criticism on the chapters as he wrote them. Merton was in turn influenced by Douglass, finding his articles and chapters stimulating and sobering. The two also shared ideas and concerns as to the direction and work of the Catholic Peace Fellowship in which they both participated.[70] That Douglass was deeply influenced by his personal relationship with Merton can perhaps best be witnessed in the naming of his son Thomas Merton.[71]

Conclusion

As we saw in the first chapter, Douglass's theology of nonviolence developed in conjunction with the changing world around him: from Cold War apocalypticism to shifts in the Catholic peace tradition to 1970s disillusionment. Equally influential were three twentieth-century figures, two of whom were also shaped by the apocalypticism and social critiques of the twentieth-century. The thought and lives of Day, Gandhi and Merton inspired Douglass and molded his ideas. Impressed by the example of Dorothy Day, he early on internalized her lived commitment to nonviolence. Her emphasis on personalism and suffering emerge as major themes in Douglass's theology of nonviolent resistance. In addition, Gandhi and Merton provided a number of important elements in Douglass's understanding of nonviolence, including the fundamental ideas of Truth and contemplative self-emptying. Most importantly, they encouraged him to explore more deeply the relationship of spirituality and nonviolent resistance. Drawing from the exemplary life of Day, and the thought of Gandhi and Merton, Douglass formulated a theology of nonviolence that strongly integrated contemplation and active resistance to injustice and evil. It is to this relationship that we now turn as we examine the themes that comprise Douglass's theology of nonviolence.

---

70. For the correspondence between Merton and Douglass, see Thomas Merton and William Henry Shannon, *The Hidden Ground of Love: The Letters of Thomas Merton on Religious Experience and Social Concerns* (New York: Farrar, Straus, Giroux, 1985), 159–67.

71. Ibid., 160.

3

Themes and Theology
Douglass's Cross and Kingdom

DRAWING FROM the intellectual and exemplary influences of Dorothy Day, Mahatma Gandhi, and Thomas Merton, James Douglass was able to develop a theology of nonviolence that moved beyond a mere pacifist ethic. Although Douglass never detailed his theology of nonviolence in any single work, one can nevertheless discern the contours of his nonviolent theology woven throughout his four main books and numerous articles. In these works, two themes emerge as the foundation of Douglass's theology of nonviolence: the theme of the Cross and that of the Kingdom. The Cross exemplifies both the humanity of Jesus in the incarnation, as well as the roles of suffering and self-emptying in redemption. The Kingdom, for Douglass, represents the greatest Reality and ultimate Truth as they exist in the reign of God. Both are vital to Douglass's understanding of nonviolence.

Although these two themes of the Cross and the Kingdom thread throughout all of his works, Douglass nuances each differently as his thought evolves. One finds, in fact, that the Cross dominates his early writings, while the Kingdom appears to take precedence in the latter. Thus, in our exploration of each theme, we will consider the various meanings of the Cross and the Kingdom as they appear chronologically in Douglass's published works. We will then examine the ways in which the various elements of the Cross and the Kingdom contribute to a cohesive "ontology of nonviolence."

The Cross: The Suffering and Self-Emptying of Humanity

Douglass's emphasis on the role of suffering and self-emptying in nonviolence served as a response to the changing historical contexts in which he lived and wrote. The political reality of the Cold War in the 1960s and the acute moral questions this raised, particularly with regard to nuclear weapons, lay heavily in the background of Douglass's first book,

The Nonviolent Cross (1968). During this time, Douglass sensed that American foreign policy, supported by the Catholic Church, had lost its way through its overwhelming concern for security. The achievement of unparalleled wealth and power in the West was matched only by its obsession with the fortification of its militaries. Warheads purportedly built in the name of protection served also to secure Western policies of exploitation throughout the world; even domestically, the accumulation of these nuclear arsenals seemed a greater priority than feeding one's own poor or ultimately valuing the lives of one's own people. "The historical pursuit of security through superior weapons," wrote Douglass, "has arrived instead at the insecurity of threatened extinction."[1] In his view, Americans were unwilling to sacrifice wealth and power and unwilling to endure the suffering that was required in order to resist the injustices of their nation and its imposition of suffering and poverty on the rest of the world. Obsessed with utility, the modern world could find no useful purpose for sacrifice. Thus Douglass looked to the Church, with its founding event in the crucifixion of Jesus, to call its people back to an embrace of suffering in the resistance evil.

Douglass saw that to the extent the Church of the fifties and sixties had capitulated to the systemic evils of the State, it had lost the meaning of the Cross. Using Carl Amery's critique of Milieu-Catholicism,[2] Douglass argued that the civic virtues embraced by the Church were not the values of the Christian tradition and could be co-opted for any number of political purposes. The message of the cross lay buried beneath the Church's public advocacy of civic virtues such as diligence and obedience that did nothing so much as secure national interests. Douglass sought to remind the Church of the significance of suffering in the Christian tradition, asserting that "suffering is the one earthly reality with which God identifies himself universally in the person of Jesus Christ."[3] Because Douglass believed that the Cross fades when church and politics mix, he encouraged the church to resist the temptation to align itself with the State. "The illusion and permanent temptation offered by Constantine continues to obscure the Christian's witness to the world," he wrote. "There is no withdrawal more corruptive of the Church than the withdrawal of the cross which masks itself as involvement, as Christ and Caesar become interchangeable com-

---

1. James Douglass, *The Non-Violent Cross*, 5.
2. See Amery, *Capitulation: The Lesson of German Catholicism*.
3. Douglass, *The Non-Violent Cross*, 54.

mitments."⁴ Instead, Douglass called the Church to take on the Cross by standing up for Truth in the face of the world's untruth.

In his reference to John XXIII and the encyclical *Pacem in Terris*, Douglass applauds the Pope as one who recognizes the importance of the Cross. Although the encyclical did not refer specifically to suffering love in its embrace of nonviolence, Douglass considered such nonviolence to be the fruit of John's own suffering—a lifelong agony of love.⁵ This stood in stark contrast to Milieu-Catholicism in which "the question of a deeply personal and therefore self-critical response to Christ does not arise."⁶ Entrenched in cultural dogma rather than welcoming the living, suffering presence of Christ, Milieu-Christianity committed incarnational heresy by incarnating "in the wrong flesh, that of the self and of the extended culture-self."⁷ As we will see, Douglass explores this problem of the "false self" more deeply in later works, as it relates to the contemplative dimension of nonviolence.

In his bold articulation of the centrality of suffering to both nonviolence and the vibrant Christian life, Douglass sought to restore living belief in the Incarnation, belief which accepts the redemptive character of the suffering Cross. "A living and scripturally founded doctrine of the Incarnation," he wrote, "will center on suffering love as the redemptive and active presence of Christ in the world."⁸ This statement reveals the crux of Douglass's thought on suffering, and may be better understood through an examination of the vital relationship between suffering and nonviolence as expressed in Douglass's earliest book, *The Nonviolent Cross*.

The Cross of Christ:
Redemption through Suffering Love

Douglass defines violence in his first book as "the willed destruction of another, or to use Simone Weil's phrase, the transformation of a man into a thing."⁹ In light of this definition, Douglass's understanding of nonviolence might be summarized as resistance to dehumanization, or more proactively, as the full realization of every person's deep humanity, revealed in the humanity of Christ. Nonviolent resistance therefore requires both love and, in

---

4. Ibid., 205.
5. Ibid., 96.
6. Ibid., 58.
7. Ibid., 54.
8. Ibid.
9. Ibid., 18.

its confrontation with the destructive powers of the world, the acceptance of suffering as a loving response to the dehumanization of violence.

In his treatment of suffering, Douglass looks to the Cross as the ultimate act of suffering (i.e., *paschal*) love. Jesus freely chose to suffer violence and evil as the supreme expression of divine love. In equating the Cross with love, Douglass ultimately equates it with redemption. "The cross," he writes, "is at once both death and life to mankind. After man's rejection of the Incarnation, God has saved him by his transformation, in and through the Resurrection, of the most awful crime in history."[10] Jesus' self-identification as the suffering servant, or *ebed Yahweh*, of the Jewish tradition revealed this most profoundly. According to Douglass, the truth revealed by *ebed Yahweh* is that salvation comes through suffering. In *The Nonviolent Cross*, Douglass traces the development of Jesus' conscious identification with *ebed Yahweh*, which culminates in the fulfillment of his earthly work as such. Douglass concludes that "essential to the definition of the Christ is suffering, rejection, and a sacrificial death."[11] If we are to know Jesus, then, we must know him in his humanity as a suffering servant, and not merely as an archetypal man or hero.

Such knowledge is not obtained by philosophical speculation, but through the subjective experience of suffering in our own lives. For it is in the experience of suffering that one shares Christ's own human experience of suffering and, therefore, redemption, as witnessed in Jesus' words in the Gospel of Mark that "whoever loses his life for my sake and the gospel's will save it" (Mark 8:35). The redemption of Christ's suffering was a result of his loving willingness to endure the world's violence. It is through our own suffering, too, when endured for the sake of love rather than violence, that we incarnate Christ and redeem both ourselves and the one who commits the violence.

Jesus' identification as *ebed Yahweh* reveals a great deal about God. In Douglass's understanding, God lives where there is suffering, though he does not perpetuate it. Rather, as shown in Christ on the Cross, God emerges from suffering as Truth and Love. "Discourse on God," wrote Douglass, "can only take on meaning with specific reference to suffering man, which is not to deny the truth of transcendence but to affirm the reality of its incarnation and continuing presence."[12] Douglass looks to Bonhoeffer in his prison cell to articulate this understanding of God's

---

10. Ibid., 226.
11. Ibid., 64.
12. Ibid., 32.

presence in suffering: "God allows himself to be edged out of the world and on to the cross. God is weak and powerless in the world, and that is exactly the way, the only way, in which he can be with us and help us. Matthew 8:17 makes it crystal clear that it is not by his omnipotence that Christ helps us, but by his weakness and suffering."[13]

Importantly, Douglass recognizes that suffering itself is evil and a consequence of sin. Love does not seek suffering, but unity and community. In the face of violence, however, love and suffering work together for its redemption. According to Douglass, "in a world in which man has first crucified his brother, love's only way to union is through the reversal of violence in suffering. And the way has been divinized. By becoming man, God has sacramentalized man's suffering so that man might become God through the cost of love. Love is the Power, but a Power incarnate on the cross."[14] It is vital to note here that it is not suffering alone, but suffering love that reveals God in our lives and unites us to the Divine. Suffering only has value if it is borne out of love, for then it becomes the ultimate expression of love. Indeed, even God endures suffering from the depths of his own love. "The cross of suffering love is God's continuing presence in each man on this earth. The Son lives today as he redeemed, in the community of peace being constantly created through the sacrifice of love."[15]

In his chapter entitled "From Gandhi to Christ," Douglass explores the significance of Christ's suffering love as revealed in Mohandas Gandhi. Recounting examples of Gandhi's fasts and prison terms, Douglass demonstrates how Gandhi's own suffering redeemed the suffering imposed upon the Indian people. The cross is redemptive, even for a non-Christian: "The cross raises the dead to the living because the cross itself is living, as Gandhi described and followed it. For Gandhi dared not think of birth without death on the cross."[16]

Suffering as Power

For Douglass, there is a sublime logic in the crucifixion which is also the logic of nonviolence. It is the paradoxical logic of God, whereby suffering is victory, and weakness is power. Much of Douglass's writing is dedicated to this alternative understanding of power as achieved through suffering.

---

13. Dietrich Bonhoeffer, *Letters and Papers from Prison*, ed. Eberhard Bethge (New York: Macmillan, 1962), 219–220. Quoted in Douglass, *The Non-Violent Cross*, 32.

14. Douglass, *The Non-Violent Cross*, 290.

15. Ibid.

16. Ibid., 75.

According to Douglass, suffering gives wisdom, which is fundamental to true power. In addition, suffering serves as a nonviolent weapon inasmuch as it provides both the endurance needed to face an oppressor and the impulse to resist. Douglass writes, "The weak have the power to endure a suffering they expect of life, and even as their suffering increases under enemy guns, their power of endurance is upheld and strengthened by the justice of their cause and by the injustice and inhumanity of the powerful."[17]

Douglass looked both to the Gandhian independence movement as well as the Vietnam War for examples of such power. The Indian populace and the Vietnamese resistance both endured a tremendous amount of suffering in their fight for justice. Douglass wrote of the power of the Vietnamese resistance:

> There is no technological equivalent, however great one's bombing capacity, for a human being who has been truly disciplined by poverty and who has accepted suffering and the expectancy of early death as a way of life. The man who has learned for years to live without comfort and without hope of a future will be prepared to tunnel beneath jungle floors or lie motionless in rice paddies, enduring the endless firepower. . . .[18]

Unfortunately, whereas the Indians grew in power by holding firm to nonviolence, the Vietnamese compromised the power they had gained through suffering by turning instead to violence. Indeed, the power of force and military might—that is to say, the power of violence—is, for Douglass, merely an illusion. Military power is not only incapable of winning the hearts and minds of people, but frequently repels and alienates them. Douglass asserts that "military power has put mankind on the cross," a place of powerlessness and deep pain.[19] Witnessing the vast military expansion of the twentieth century, Douglass believed that the knowledge of real power—paradoxically realized in the 'powerlessness' of nonviolence—was all but lost in the modern world. Humanity had not yet embraced the lesson of the cross, unable to see that real power lies in suffering love rather than force. Douglass uses Gandhi's language of Truth in his explanation of real power:

> Power is revealed not as violence, which destroys, nor even simply as suffering, which endures, but as Truth, which resists injustice through voluntary suffering, and as Love, which in that suffer-

17. Ibid., 14.
18. James Douglass, *Resistance and Contemplation: The Way of Liberation*, 31–32.
19. Douglass, *The Non-Violent Cross*, 6.

ing resistance opens victim to executioner and thus raises their relationship from the level of objects, passive and active, to that of persons, confronting and confronted. . . . Truth can exert its enormous power only by being incarnated in the humility and apparent weakness of suffering Love. . . . Truth is powerless without suffering Love as its medium.[20]

As the medium of Truth, suffering Love resists untruth, powerful in that it is God's work rather than our own.

Suffering as Resisting Untruth

The resistance of untruth is a vital component in Douglass's nonviolence, and the primary reason for suffering love. For Douglass, untruth can be experienced in injustice, oppression, exploitation, and violence, among other things. To resist such untruths, one needs to adhere to one's conscience and serve others through love and sacrifice. Violent resistance, while potentially effective in the short-term, only prolongs untruth. Nonviolent resistance, on the other hand, serves Truth by incarnating Love. Yet nonviolently resisting violent and unjust power structures inevitably results in suffering, both internally and externally. Resistance causes internal suffering because it demands an inner transformation through which one releases one's claims on the ways of the world. Douglass explains this "passage into fire" in *The Nonviolent Cross*:

> The radical change which is revolution means change affecting the very nature of man in the world, inasmuch as man's nature has become conformed through the ages to structures and institutions radically incapable of meeting the needs of the human family today. . . . Revolution means transformation because man deformed by such structures and institutions must pass into a fire of truth consuming his very nature as he has built it up—a nature fragmented in body and committed in spirit to a power which is impotent . . . .[21]

Resistance also results in external suffering as those in power continue to protect untruth by the use of force and intimidation. For Douglass, this explains why Jesus warned his disciples to expect the suffering of poverty and persecution.

Throughout his first book, Douglass identifies nonviolence with the resistance of untruth, an untruth that meets us in dehumanizing systems

---

20. Ibid., 19.
21. Ibid., 21–22.

of injustice, violence, exploitation, and oppression. Nonviolent action embraces the enemy by lovingly enduring suffering, thereby redeeming the inflicted violence and transforming it into love. Such nonviolence participates sacramentally in Christ's own suffering and redemption of human violence, incarnating God through our own human acts of love. For Douglass, then, the suffering of nonviolence is deeply redemptive, incarnational, and powerful. It was these ideas with regard to suffering and to a theology of nonviolence that served later as a foundation for the continual development of Douglass's thought, leading to a greater emphasis on contemplation in subsequent works.

The Cross as Self-Emptying

Douglass wrote his second book, *Resistance and Contemplation* (1972), in the latter years of the Vietnam War, after the assassination of Martin Luther King, Jr. and Robert Kennedy, and during the gradual decline of the once-vibrant peace movement that we explored in the first chapter. *Resistance and Contemplation* responds to the era's extinguished vision of peace, and to the resulting sense of hopelessness. Douglass saw that the collapse of hope in the remarkable young people of this generation was something like Sisyphus' stone now rolling inexorably backward.[22] The once hopeful and vigorous were left feeling powerless and full of despair. In addition, earlier proponents of nonviolence had begun to reconsider whether violence was not indeed necessary to confront the world's injustices.

Surrounded by this sense of hopelessness, Douglass turned his attention to the importance of spirituality in sustaining nonviolent resistance. In his article "Non-violence and Metanoia" (1974), Douglass recounts the deepening of this spiritual dimension of his nonviolence during the Vietnam War.

> The suffering from the war continued to be so overwhelming that one clearly could and had to go deeper, infinitely deeper, in one's life toward an unrealized center of grace out of which an altogether new and transforming kind of non-violence could then arise. The Gospels called such a possibility *metanoia*. . . .
>
> I believe that 'non-violence reconsidered' after the experiences of the '60s can only mean the continuing search for that far deeper center of the inner dimension of non-violence, which would be

---

22. Douglass, *Resistance and Contemplation: The Way of Liberation*, 49.

expressed less in action than in transformation, whose discovery is the spiritual (and political) imperative of our nuclear end-time.[23]

In reconsidering the inner dimension of nonviolence, Douglass interpreted the despair of his generation as the requisite suffering and powerlessness that accompanies true nonviolence. In the depths of impotence and hopelessness, wrote Douglass, one discovers the seedbed for conversion and the freedom to throw oneself fully into the service of God. By enduring the necessary divestment of hope, we begin to understand that liberation extends beyond mere political resistance. True liberation is to be without political and social props and to therefore have to face oneself alone. This is the contemplative element of the cross that "begins with a sharp perception of our rock-bottom poverty and powerlessness."[24]

In *Resistance and Contemplation*, Douglass draws on his studies of Merton and newly discovered ideas from Eastern religions,[25] to include this more contemplative dimension of self-emptying in his understanding of nonviolent suffering. While the theme of the cross of suffering remains critical to Douglass's understanding of nonviolence, Douglass broadens it to include the more spiritual dimension of the "emptied self." We turn therefore to explore the importance of self-emptying in Douglass's theology of the nonviolent cross. By doing so, we will obtain the necessary foundation to treat the relationship of contemplation and nonviolence in the following chapter.

"The paradigm of liberation is the cross and the empty tomb, crucifixion and resurrection, suffering love and transforming power," asserts Douglass.[26] The value of suffering lies less in what it accomplishes than in the extent to which it transforms our being. Love willing to suffer changes who we are in our deepest selves—compassionate people who are more concerned with the other than with ourselves. Our altered being reflects the presence of Christ within. "Deeper than any repossession of the land

23. James Douglass, "Non-Violence and Metanoia," *Katallagete* 5, no. 2 (1974): 29.

24. Douglass, *Resistance and Contemplation: The Way of Liberation*, 51.

25. Douglass uses the two Taoist notions of "The Way" and "Yin-Yang" complimentarity in his chapter entitled "Yin-Yang of Resistance and Contemplation." The Way also has a strong presence in his article entitled, "Prison," *Katallagete* (1972). As we will see in the following chapter, Douglass also finds the Zen notion of emptiness to be valuable in his emphasis on renunciation and contemplation. He looks to Merton's *Mystics and Zen Masters* (1967), and *Zen and the Birds of Appetite*, (New York: New Directions, 1968), as well as D.T. Suzuki's *Essays in Zen Buddhism* (New York: Grove Press, 1961). Cf. Douglass's chapter "Yin-Yang of Resistance and Contemplation," as well as later essays such as "Thomas Merton's Glimpse of the Kingdom," (1981).

26. Douglass, *Resistance and Contemplation: The Way of Liberation*, 30.

by the people is the renewal of their humanity in a struggle which is truthful, loving and life-giving. Humanity needs that struggle even more than it needs a victorious end, for the struggle is the victory."[27] For Douglass, the struggle for liberation takes place as much within a person as without, and it is within that the greatest change takes place. Significantly, Douglass emphasizes that the inner suffering which transforms one's being cannot be realized through active resistance alone. Indeed, a lasting commitment to nonviolent resistance requires that one be grounded in the personal suffering of an emptied self.

This necessary inner movement of self-emptying emerges as a significant aspect of suffering in *Resistance and Contemplation* as well as in other published articles from the same period.[28] Without ever concretely defining it, Douglass uses the term "self-emptying" to suggest a renunciation of self-interest and attachment to the ego. The self being emptied here bears resemblance to Merton's "false self," an illusory, autonomous "I" which serves to mask the emptiness at the core of our being.[29] To empty this self, then, is to renounce self-interest, self-righteousness, and self-justification, all of which are attempts to deny the fundamental hollowness within. According to Douglass, a truly emptied self will experience an intensely painful recognition of one's own poverty and powerlessness. One may witness such powerlessness in the case of Jesus, alone in the wilderness or abandoned on the cross. Douglass writes of Jesus' exemplary powerlessness:

> On a dark night Jesus cried out in the center of his valley, 'My God, my God, why have you forsaken me?' The void was answered with silence. Yet the dark silence like that of Gethsemane, was the most liberating answer possible, for it emptied Jesus of any conceivable claim to power, rendered him the most powerless of creatures, handed his life over completely to the Father: "Father, into your hands I commit my spirit." On the cross Jesus experienced a valley

---

27. Ibid.

28. See Douglass, "Prison" (1972), "Non-Violence and Metanoia" (1974), and "Thomas Merton's Glimpse of the Kingdom" (1981).

29. Interestingly, Douglass rarely employs Merton's term of "false self." We can witness it briefly in his 1981 essay, "Thomas Merton's Glimpse of the Kingdom," and in the 1996 essay, "Civil Disobedience as Prayer." In his other works, Douglass rarely clarifies what "self" is being emptied, and might have benefited from a more frequent reference to Merton's "false self." See Thomas Merton, *New Seeds of Contemplation* (New York: New Directions, 1972), 6–46.

whose emptiness was total, thus freeing him for his total gift of life in death to the Father.[30]

According to Douglass, we need to know the poverty of our autonomous selves and our deep alienation in order to unite with the Divine. Only in knowing the pain of separation are we able to overcome it. When we finally embrace our alienated existential situation as a part of our cross, that is, when we are able to contemplate our own poverty, we will find then that we are free from the constraints of our illusory selves.

Nevertheless, Douglas says something more here: the goal of self-renunciation is not merely to recognize our own impoverishment. Douglass emphasizes that we are liberated through such kenotic poverty to experience true *metanoia*, or turning toward God. Equating renunciation with emptiness and becoming 'zero,' terms used by Zen practitioners and Thomas Merton, Douglass emphasizes that the ultimate goal of renunciation is a movement towards God. "Renunciation empties one out for the sake of faith," he wrote.[31] Such emptiness is where metanoia is birthed. To turn towards God with all of our being we must first lose the naïve and illusory faith that only serves to buttress our egos. Only through the "wrenching emptiness of man's self-renunciation" can one know the presence of God. Through self-emptying, we are unified with the One and therefore able to witness from a place of truth and love.[32] "It is only then," wrote Douglass, "after letting go of a grasping self, that a man is prepared to join Jesus in resisting the powers—'to take up his cross and follow me'; to trial, to imprisonment, death; to whatever these may mean in the living reality of one's own resistance."[33] Only in the dark night can we acknowledge the evil that must be resisted. True resistance, then, is a process of *metanoia* and is born from this kenotic place of self-emptying.

Resistance realized through the emptied self reaches its apex in death. Indeed, resisting evil and violence to the point of death reveals an utterly liberated self. As Douglass remarks, "Death as the gift of self in and to Love is the ultimately liberating act which overcomes evil and makes life wholly and finally affirmative."[34] Although death certainly may be the result of divisive evil, through love it can be transformed into a gift of the self for others and for God. As the greatest expression of kenosis, and therefore as

30. Douglass, *Resistance and Contemplation: The Way of Liberation*, 190–91.
31. Ibid., 60.
32. Ibid., 59.
33. Ibid., 60.
34. Ibid., 190.

a gift of love, death most fully unites us with God. While this transformation of death is most perfectly realized in the crucifixion of Jesus, others have been able to transform death into the giving of life as well. Gandhi and the Satyagrahis, many of whom gave their lives for Indian liberation, were prime examples for Douglass. Douglass explains:

> Satyagraha is the truth of being in action. As a revolutionary force, it has no limits except the reluctance of its practitioners to sacrifice themselves wholly to the truth. . . . Gandhi's description of the way of the satyagraha calls to mind the early Christians' understanding of Jesus' way of poverty, a way of complete self-emptying to the point of accepting death on a cross. . . . In the Christian context, then, the explosive power of satyagraha would be the exaltation of man by God realized through man's becoming one with Jesus' complete self-emptying on the cross, thereby becoming one with being.[35]

Death and self-emptying are not merely extreme expressions of resistance, or even effective means for the liberation of the self; they are redemptive acts. Accepting death out of love for one's neighbor, or for the sake of Truth, serves most importantly to unite one with God and by incarnating the Divine, to redeem the world's violence.

Douglass shares his own experience of the liberating potential of suffering and self-emptying in an article entitled "Prison," published in the journal *Katallagete* the same year as *Resistance and Contemplation*. He understands prisons as "techniques for America's violent control of her rebellious poor" and "raw power in the service of a ruling class."[36] More importantly, however, he finds that prisons are the ultimate examples of technique: the suppression of humanity for the sake of rational efficiency. As such, the penal system attempts to dehumanize the incarcerated, drawing them further away from reality and their true selves. As a system of violence, however, prisons can be potentially liberating when willingly endured for the sake of Truth. Douglass pays tribute to Gandhi's belief that prison can lead to liberation when he writes that "the cell door is the door to freedom because once I am prepared to walk through that door I have nothing to fear."[37]

Threatened with prison himself for committing acts of civil disobedience, Douglass finds his own sense of freedom through a willingness to accept the consequences of his actions. In addition, by enduring such con-

---

35. Ibid., 145–46.
36. Douglass, "Prison," 53.
37. Ibid., 52.

finement consciously and contemplatively, he realizes his own attachment to effectiveness and technique and is forced to suffer without any promise of positive consequences. Prison is liberating, writes Douglass, because it "repudiates in an act of Being the self-confinement of technique which is the most profound form of our common bondage."[38] Facing a potential prison term of months and perhaps even years, however, he is not certain how long he will be able to endure such a sentence "and still come up singing freedom." He knows, however, that such uncertainty is an important element of redemptive suffering, bringing him to the depths of powerlessness and poverty, and opening him to God. To be completely empty is to be without guarantees of victory or even redemption. "I believe," Douglass writes, "that prison, like death on a cross, can in faith open a way into a valley of silence where life flows without ceasing."[39]

This emphasis on self-emptying intensifies in subsequent articles, and particularly in his third book, *Lightning East to West* (1983), where his language reflects a more inward, spiritual focus with terms such as ego-crucifixion and consideration of Carl Jung's 'shadow.' In *Lightning East to West*, Douglass relates how through his own experience of marriage and civil disobedience he learned the importance of such self-emptying. He discovered that the experienced loss of control and darkness were prerequisites for nonviolent transformation and growth in Truth. "In a sense," Douglass writes, "no one can choose *metanoia*. One can only choose *metanoia*'s situation of powerlessness, a point in one's life whereby one is exposed simply and nakedly to *metanoia*'s ruthless destruction of self-images."[40]

Douglass uses wilderness as a metaphor for the self-emptying and ego-crucifixion that results in conversion: "The wilderness exposes one to the experience of powerlessness, to a sense of absolute dependence on forces beyond oneself. One goes into the solitude of wilderness to pray because it shatters self-sufficient pride and forces one to acknowledge whatever can remain hidden elsewhere."[41] Jesus' wilderness experience serves as the ultimate example. According to Douglass, in the wilderness Jesus would have had to acknowledge his shadow and emptiness, and it would have been ego-shattering. Thus the question confronts all who desire to act with

---

38. Ibid., 54.
39. Ibid.
40. James Douglass, *Lightning East to West*, 62.
41. Ibid., 32.

the force of Truth and the love of God: How deeply will I acknowledge my own emptiness?[42]

Suffering as Liberation

As we have seen, the suffering that Douglass finds vital to nonviolence is both a cross of resistance and a cross of self-emptying. Much like in his first book, *The Non-Violent Cross,* Douglass's later works again stress the imperative of nonviolent resistance to social, political, and economic injustice. In *Resistance and Contemplation,* he refers specifically to the injustices suffered in Vietnam and other Third World countries, where the policies and affluence of the United States help to perpetuate continued poverty and exploitation. He sharply critiques the capitalist assumption that it is perfectly normal for six percent of the world's population to own sixty percent of its wealth.[43] Douglass calls Americans to resist their nation's political, economic, and military exploitation and oppression. A half-hearted commitment, he emphasizes, will not suffice. To liberate our neighbors from oppression and ourselves as oppressors, we must be willing to serve the Truth at any cost. The oft-repeated question convicts the reader: "A way of liberation passes through fire. To what extent am I willing to pass through that fire myself?"[44] It is the fire of suffering that lies in the way of liberation. "Our talk of liberation," Douglass writes, "becomes serious when we realize sharply that we are saved by the liberator's blood only when we allow it to mix with our own."[45] As we have seen, however, the fire is also one of purification and self-emptying, a paschal fire.

To embrace both ideas of active suffering love and contemplative self-emptying, Douglass employed the term 'liberation'. Nonviolence, he wrote, is the way of liberation. One's freedom is two-fold: a political and economic liberation, realized in resistance to systemic oppression, and a spiritual liberation realized in the emptying of the self before God. As we will see in the following chapter, both aspects of liberation, like the horizontal and vertical arms of the Cross, were intrinsically tied to one another. This Cross stood at the center of Douglass's vision for both political resistance and kenotic transformation—a fundamental element of his understanding of nonviolence.

---

42. Ibid., 33.
43. Douglass, *Resistance and Contemplation: The Way of Liberation,* 27.
44. Ibid., 45.
45. Ibid., 25.

Clarifying the relationship of nonviolence, suffering, and redemption, Douglass explored the idea of liberation as the unifying factor in all three. He believed the fruit of suffering to be liberation—a liberation from both personal and social bondage. Liberation, informed by nonviolence and its requisite suffering, results in both personal redemption and the redemption of society. "Liberation is the redemption of man from his violence, a socially and personally pervasive violence. . . . Liberation is the cross of self-emptying, suffering, and non-violent love which moves one to faith, and to a deeper humanity."[46]

We have explored the various ways in which the cross is of vital importance to Douglass's understanding of nonviolence. Douglass's attention to emptiness and suffering, however, while important, is not the focal point of his works, as becomes increasingly apparent in later writings such as *Lightning East to West*. Emptiness, for Douglass, is important inasmuch as it leads to oneness with God and a realization of Reality. We need ego-renunciation in order to see the interpenetration of inner and outer worlds, to glimpse the Truth and its capacity to embrace the world. Douglass articulates the ultimate purpose of self-emptying when he writes,

> The cross is the ultimate statement in community of the truth discovered in the wilderness: That complete emptying is complete oneness, that perfect death is perfect life. . . . The cross of suffering love and service to others is the communal fulfillment of oneness in the wilderness. The cross is that loss of self where the unity of inner and outer worlds . . . gets lived and suffered into a complete and total oneness.[47]

Sacrifice, suffering, and self-emptying are meaningful only to the extent that they lead us to the ultimate Reality. Douglass refers to Reality as the essence of God's Kingdom, a Kingdom that breaks into the world to the extent that we participate in it. This notion of the Kingdom surfaces as a major theme, primarily in Douglass's later works, as he focuses on the ontological reality of nonviolence, realized through the cross of self-emptying and manifesting the Kingdom in this world.

---

46. Ibid., 30.
47. Douglass, *Lightning East to West*, 53.

The Kingdom: the Manifestation of Truth, Reality, and the One

Despite the many terms Douglass employs to speak about the nonviolent presence and power of God, they may all be considered under the rubric of 'the Kingdom.' Indeed, the realization of the Kingdom of God, in and through sacrificial and self-emptying nonviolence, is the thrust of Douglass's later writing. The Kingdom provides meaning to both contemplation and resistance, and is the ultimate end to which nonviolence aspires. It is therefore necessary to explore the contours of Douglass's understanding of the Kingdom of God and its relationship to his ontology of nonviolence, but to do so adequately we must first consider the different terms he employed to speak about God.

In using religious and cultural sources outside of the Christian tradition, Douglass adopted terms for God that do not restrict the notion of the transcendent to a traditionally Christian interpretation. He primarily uses three terms to refer in different ways to God: Truth, Reality, and One. The notion of Truth appears throughout Douglass's writings, although he primarily employs the term in his earlier books. His use of 'Truth' is indebted to Gandhi who adopted the term because, unlike terms such as love, "I never found a double meaning in connection with truth, and not even atheists had demurred to the necessity of the power of Truth."[48] For Douglass, Truth allowed one to speak in a secular fashion about God, because God's presence could not be separated from Truth. Again, Douglass looks to Gandhi for his understanding of Truth, and the relationship to God is apparent: "Truth," Gandhi writes, "gives perennial joy . . . . Truth is Knowledge also. It is Life. You feel vitality in you when you have got Truth in you. Again, it gives you bliss. It is a permanent thing of which you cannot be robbed. You may be sent to the gallows, or put to torture, but if you have Truth in you, you will experience inner joy."[49] Douglass expands on this description of Truth, naming it as a timeless and disembodied transcendence which is also simultaneously present. Truth, for Douglass and Gandhi both, exists in the ontological relationship between God and Man.[50]

Douglass adopts Gandhi's distinction between absolute Truth and the disparate truths that individuals hold. Truth, he writes, "cannot be identified simply with one's own position. . . ." One must maintain a commitment

---

48. Mahatma Gandhi, *God Is Truth*, ed. Anand T. Hingorani, [2nd] ed. (Bombay: Bharatiya Vidya Bhavan, 1962). Quoted in Douglass, *The Non-Violent Cross*, 35.

49. Gandhi, *God Is Truth*. Quoted in Douglass, *The Non-Violent Cross*, 35–36.

50. Douglass, *The Non-Violent Cross*, 90.

to Truth without claiming it prematurely; that is, one must adhere to what one believes to be true while constantly seeking to advance in Truth through openness and humility. In treating the conflict of truths that arises among opponents, Douglass asserts that "Real truth is not our side victorious in any sense, but the mutual victory of both opponents over the conflict between them."[51] Adhering to truth always entails seeking the good of all over the desires of the self. As such, truth is compromised by violence: "However great the pressures arguing for violence," Douglass stresses, "a gun remains a very imperfect means of defending or serving the truth, and the truth is inevitably compromised and obscured by its use."[52]

Indeed, uncompromised Truth has its own strength. As noted earlier, among communities suffering and resisting injustice, the truth of one's cause can serve as the basis of one's strength, as witnessed among the Vietnamese during the war and among the Indians during their movement for independence. "The power of truth is the power to convince a man, to change his mind and heart, to turn him in the direction of justice and humanity." Douglass continues, "The Truth which Gandhi identified with God . . . seeks the liberation of both sides, poor and wealthy, from the common bondage of an inhuman relationship."[53] This is the reason why Truth's medium, God's medium, is not violence but a more loving human life.

As we have seen, Truth, for both Douglass and Gandhi, extends far beyond any factual correctness or right behavior. Truth is divine, participating in the Goodness of God, and therefore oriented toward justice and humanity. Douglass also emphasizes that Truth is very real, a power that can be experienced more than a mere concept to be contemplated. The importance of Truth's reality increases in Douglass's works as he turns his attention to its ontological transcendence and simultaneous presence in the world. Indeed, as his thought evolves, Douglass focuses on Reality as a crucial way of understanding God. One finds, for example, that he employs the term Reality frequently in his later work, *Lightning East to West*, as the concept becomes essential to his theology of nonviolence.

Nonviolence, for Douglass, requires absolute trust in the wisdom of God as well as a belief that the divine presence can be made manifest through our selfless suffering and commitment to the Truth. Douglass therefore makes the Reality of God a major theme in *Lightning East to*

---

51. Ibid., 89.
52. Douglass, *Resistance and Contemplation: The Way of Liberation*, 34.
53. Ibid., 42.

West. Equating Reality with what Jesus called 'the Father,' Douglass believes that "there is a loving, caring will at the center of reality which is as objective and concrete as a physical law. To experiment in its truth is to discover and confirm its reality."[54] The Gospel introduces us to a new reality through the story of Jesus, who Douglass asserts first passed into the reality of the kingdom through his ego-crucifixion. "The same baptism of fire is required of us to discover the kingdom's reality today," he writes.[55]

Only through *metanoia* are we able to see Reality, present spiritually and physically throughout this world. God as Reality stands in opposition to the illusions we so frequently mistake for Truth. Conversion reveals that we were previously blind to Reality, as it shatters our illusions of power and the independent ego. As Douglass explains, "The reason for our blindness to Reality, and to the kingdom of a new world present in it, is that the world we think we see is only a view, a description of the world . . . and the view a reflection of the ego."[56] For Douglass, only God is Real, and it is this search for Reality which defines all nonviolent action.

Finally, in speaking of God, Douglass also employs the term "the One." Used less frequently than either Truth or Reality, the One nevertheless reveals God as the unifying essence of all life. According to Douglass, the One emerges in our embrace of poverty and renunciation of power, as it reasserts "a power which is over no one but within all."[57] As Douglass writes in *Resistance and Contemplation*, "In a revolution through solitude the One is the many, the many satyagrahis who fan out into a death-infested society and reignite the fire of unity, the One rekindled in the many beyond who make up the people and whose power lies in a rediscovery of their unity."[58] Nonviolence unifies both oppressor and oppressed by recognizing the presence of the One in all. To practice nonviolence is to participate in the One, as well as to know the Truth and open the world to Reality. Nonviolence is, in essence, union with God.

Having considered Douglass's vision of God as Truth, Reality, and the One, we are now able to obtain a more comprehensive understanding of the theme of God's Kingdom. Douglass draws the foundation for his notion of the Kingdom from Scripture. As he writes in *The Nonviolent Coming of God*, "If we recall here Q's Inaugural Sermon and Luke's Sermon

---

54. Douglass, *Lightning East to West*, 2.
55. Ibid., 3.
56. Ibid., 61.
57. Douglass, *Resistance and Contemplation: The Way of Liberation*, 147.
58. Ibid.

on the Plain, the specific kingdom Jesus is talking about is one in which the ruler is a parent who 'showers kindness on the ungrateful and the evil.' The power in this kingdom is love, especially love of enemies."[59] According to Douglass, the Kingdom of God represents the manifestation of God's reign and love in the world. Put another way, the Kingdom is the revelation of God's own being in the world as "the partnership of God and man in history."[60] The Kingdom can be witnessed everywhere Truth is present. It is the emergence of Reality in our own consciousness and the movement of all into the One. While Douglass refers to the Kingdom in a multitude of ways, two symbols of the reign of God dominate Douglass's thought: the Kingdom as a Revolution realized through resistance and experiments with Truth, and the Kingdom as a New Humanity, realized in the Second Coming. Both of these understandings deserve extensive consideration, and so it is to the Revolution and New Humanity that we now turn.

The Emergence of the Kingdom as Revolution

Douglass first reveals the idea of the Christian revolution in *The Non-Violent Cross*. Interpreting Jesus' life and crucifixion as the beginning of the revolution, Douglass looks to Jesus both as a model and a force in its continuation. After contrasting Jesus' own behavior with that of the Zealot revolutionaries of his time, Douglass writes, "Jesus resisted evil with an intensity which revealed the uselessness and irrelevance of violence, and this resistance of love constitutes the Christian Revolution."[61] This Christian Revolution is the ongoing revolution of peace and truth, capable of toppling the existing power structures which bring so much suffering and violence to the world.

In this first book, Douglass's emphasizes the importance of nonviolent resistance in the Christian revolution. He sees it as an imperative of the nuclear age to participate in the revolution by adopting Jesus' way of suffering resistance to the unconscionable exploitation and militarization of the state. "To the human family's threatened murder by nuclear weapons," he writes, "and to its ongoing murder by privilege and indifference, the response of the human conscience is 'No!' In such a world, revolution is not a question and a possibility. It is an obligation and a necessity."[62]

---

59. James Douglass, *The Nonviolent Coming of God*, 155.
60. Douglass, *The Non-Violent Cross*, 27.
61. Ibid., 192.
62. Ibid., 8.

Nothing less will do than a full commitment to Christ's way of compassion and justice, as expressed in suffering resistance.

The Non-Violent Cross emphasizes revolutionary resistance primarily in terms of Christians' relationship to the state. Douglass is dissatisfied with the two traditional patterns of church/state relationships. On the one hand, sectarian withdrawal does not respond adequately to social injustices and political violence. On the other hand, aligning oneself with the world's power structures in order to impose Christian values is equally inadequate.[63] For Douglass, true revolution emerges from solidarity with the powerless, witnessing to the truth of Christ by standing firm in resistance to political untruth. "The founder of Christianity," Douglass explains, "promised not that the Church would convert the world but that it would endure until the end of time precisely as a sign of contradiction." He elaborates further on the proper role of the church community:

> The community of belief foreseen by Christ is neither triumphant by converting and dominating the world nor sectarian by withdrawing from it. It is a Christian community living at the center of the world in the form of Christ's decisive confrontation with that world—a cross of suffering, redemptive love.[64]

Thinly veiled in the above comment is Douglass's lifelong opposition to Church support of American militarization in the twentieth century. It is the illusory temptation offered by Constantine, he writes, that "continues to obscure the Christian's witness to the world and to the modern state in particular."[65] The true Christian revolution is not achieved by withdrawal or capitulation, but by witnessing to the truth through resistance.

Revolution, according to Douglass, is a radical change that affects the very nature of the human in the world. Because we are so conformed to surrounding structures and institutions, revolution is not simply a political change, but the transformation of who we are—the power of resurrection. Again, Douglass looks to the depths of suffering for the ultimate transformation required for genuine revolution. "The seed of revolution is suffering: the endurance of suffering is both the impulse and the potential strength of those who must and will rise up for a just and human order."[66] As discussed earlier, such suffering gives those who desire a changed order a power that extends beyond the power of any military or oppressive force. Douglass

63. Ibid., 204.
64. Ibid., 204–5.
65. Ibid., 205.
66. Ibid., 13.

stresses, however, the necessity for suffering to be "informed by something beyond itself in order to fulfill itself and make the revolution real."[67]

This revolutionary transformation, informed by the power of God, is the coming of the Kingdom. The revolutionary responds to her present circumstances in a torn world with nonviolent, suffering love, and as a result, transforms both herself and the world. "The revolutionary has no other choice in love than to seek with his whole being a new heaven and a new earth."[68] Seeing the world with the compassionate eyes of God, one cannot choose complacency. One is also unable to respond with hatred or violence, opting instead to respect the humanity of the enemy through suffering love and forgiveness. This was the revolution that began with Jesus and which continues through his presence in our own experience of the cross. Through this revolution, violence is redeemed and the Kingdom is revealed in the form of a new heaven and earth.

Douglass continues to explicate the Kingdom through the concept of revolution in *Resistance and Contemplation*. In the chapter entitled "The Revolution is the Kingdom," Douglass emphasizes that the nonviolent revolution requires liberation from attachment to the fruit of one's actions. Such liberation is found paradigmatically in symbolic action. Symbolic action involves the performance of revolutionary acts for the sheer purpose of witnessing to the Truth. The meaning of such actions are not dependent on results and those involved are thereby able to opt out of the power struggle frequently required to institute effective change. Symbolic action is, rather, a testament to the presence and power of the Kingdom, whose results are often hidden and yet exceed our own expectations and capabilities. Douglass draws upon three historical examples of symbolic action that, instead of being distracted with effective results, served only to witness to the Truth: Gandhi's Salt March, Jesus' "symbolic takeover" of the Temple in Jerusalem, and Daniel and Phillip Berrigan's burning of draft files with seven others in Catonsville. Douglass finds that all three "were symbols of revolution, symbols of invitation to the people. The actions were living statements which invited the people to realize their own power, if they would only do likewise and act in concert."[69]

Like the emptying of the self, the renunciation of the fruits of action liberates a person to act solely in the service of Truth. Douglass learned the significance of such renunciation from Gandhi who himself understood

---

67. Ibid.
68. Ibid., 8.
69. Douglass, *Resistance and Contemplation: The Way of Liberation*, 82.

liberation as detachment from the rewards of action. "Renunciation was the core of Gandhi's inner discipline, the heart of the doctrine of satyagraha,"[70] Douglass explains. While we should not be indifferent to the results of our actions, nevertheless if we do not *require* a certain end, we are free to throw ourselves into an action as the goal itself. Douglass clarifies this thought in relation to Gandhi's *swaraj,* or liberation movement: "The point is that renunciation of the end of national liberation, a brooding over which will only result in frustration and violence or a loss of faith and nerve, frees one for total absorption into its means."[71]

Douglass emphasizes that truthful action should be both the means and the ends of our effort. The way of Jesus, for example, is both an ontological reality to be sought after, and the path on which we move. Likewise, the renunciation of the self is both the goal of our striving and the means of our action, for it is through renunciation that we meet God. According to Douglass, "for Jesus like Gandhi (who looked to Jesus as a model for the satyagrahi), the way of renunciation was for the sake of the kingdom, which is not tomorrow's national objective but a constant personal and communal possibility."[72] God's presence in the kingdom is not some future aspiration, but a potential reality at every moment. As such, one cannot expect to compromise the means for a desired end and still work for the kingdom—the kingdom, after all, is realized in the means. Douglass cites Jacques Maritain's assertion that the means are "in a sense the end in the process of becoming."[73] "The means, for Jesus," continues Douglass, "is God. God's kingdom is not only the end. God's kingdom is the means, present and waiting."[74] If the revolution is to remain rooted in the kingdom, it must take a "living" form; that is, it must express itself in its means as well as its ends.[75]

Coincident with his high evaluation of truthful means, Douglass offers a strong critique of 'technique' in a number of his writings.[76] In these works, he describes technique as "an abstract instrument of control

---

70. Ibid., 94.

71. Ibid.

72. Ibid., 103.

73. Quoted in Douglass, *The Nonviolent Coming of God*, 154.

74. Ibid.

75. Douglass, *The Non-Violent Cross*, 9.

76. His critique of technique is particularly sharp in the chapter entitled "Psychedelic Contemplation" in *Resistance and Contemplation,* as well as in the article "On Transcending Technique" published in *Katallagete* (1970).

in which there is no living truth, only man's will to power."⁷⁷ War, pollution, and propaganda are all examples of technique, where effectiveness and efficiency take priority over human value, and the ends are severed from the means. Dehumanization, indeed, is a frequent consequence of technique, as can be witnessed in the great excitement over increasingly advanced weapons and their killing 'efficiency'. Douglass writes, "Men commit acts of violence and injustice against other men only to the extent that they do not regard them as fully human. Non-violent resistance seeks to persuade the aggressor to recognize in his victim the humanity they have in common, which when recognized makes violence impossible."⁷⁸ Technique, then, predisposes us to violence in its dehumanization of the other. The concern for efficiency supersedes any thought as to whether the action might be right or wise.

For Douglass, technique stands in opposition to the Kingdom because it tries to bring about desired ends through endless manipulation and disregard of the means. Furthermore, technique may be considered a type of spiritual enslavement, as one is only concerned with accomplishing desired ends rather than living out Truth through the Spirit of God. The need to get what we want stands in contrast to what Merton describes as "learning the ways of the spirit and grace, being ready and open to respond to the unpredictable working of a God whose ways are 'not our ways.'"⁷⁹ Christ himself was the victim of technique—the cross as means of suppression—yet he confronted it not with effective violence but with the loving Spirit of the Kingdom. Drawing much of his thought from Jacques Ellul's *The Technological Society* (1965), Douglass writes, "If in the modern world the most dangerous form of determinism is the technological phenomenon, man's permanent source of freedom is still, as Ellul also states, the life of the Holy Spirit. Only the living truth of the Holy Spirit is capable of transcending technique and freeing man."⁸⁰

For Douglass, to transcend technique is to live truthfully in the present, in means as well as ends, and thereby participate in the revolution of the Kingdom. Gandhi describes this renunciation of fruits and focused attention to Reality as "experiments in truth," a designation frequently employed by Douglass to refer to one's participation in the Kingdom. "An

77. James Douglass, "On Transcending Technique," *Katallagete,* Winter (1970): 51.

78. Douglass, *The Non-Violent Cross,* 71.

79. Thomas Merton, "Renewal and Discipline in the Monastic Life," *Cistercian Studies* V, no. 1 (1970): 6–7. Quoted in Douglass, *Resistance and Contemplation: The Way of Liberation,* 121.

80. Douglass, "On Transcending Technique," 51.

experiment in truth," writes Douglass, "is an effort to realize God's presence as truth *both in and through* a particular action."[81] Every situation is open to numerous possibilities for participating in Truth, and experiments involve probing and discerning these possibilities. According to Douglass, an experiment in truth "draws no pre-established lines concerning the ability of man to grow in truth, but tries instead to open him progressively and self-critically to the Power latent in and transcendent in each second of existence. . . . It is contemplation in action, a search for and expression of truth in the most spiritually resistant areas of life."[82]

Douglass views experiments in truth as necessary to the realization of the Kingdom. Through such experiments, one discerns whether an action would be appropriate for the hastening of the Kingdom, as well as appropriate once the Kingdom itself is established.[83] He considers such an experiment to be a *Mitzvah*, or in the Jewish tradition, a divinely commanded deed. Douglass looks to Jesus who, along with Gandhi, serves as a "symbol and prophet of the kingdom of Reality," by experimenting with truth through day-to-day self-emptying service. As exemplified in the life of Jesus, experiments in truth contribute to a sustained way of *metanoia* because they open us to a complete faith and participation in Reality. According to Douglass, Jesus himself had to discover absolute trust in God through experiments of doubt and darkness. The period of fasting in the wilderness exhibits Jesus' own experiment with truth. Rejecting the three temptations of power offered by the devil, Jesus accepted powerlessness as a way to Reality and placed his faith in God. Jesus freely chose death on the cross as a continuation of this experiment. One cannot merely speculate about the coming of the Kingdom through faith—it must be experienced. Jesus did not try out the cross to see if his faith would work, explains Douglass. The Son of Man had to relinquish himself to the demands of Truth, and trust that through such an experience, the Kingdom would be realized.

Experiments with truth involve a "disciplined probing of the outer wall of one's limitations, where the pure grace of Reality extends the truth beyond any individual's capacity to see the way forward and confers on that truth an objective power of change."[84] Douglass believes Jesus exhorted us to probe our limitations and rely on the power of God in Matthew 7:7:

81. Douglass, *The Non-Violent Cross*, 44.
82. Ibid., 45.
83. Douglass draws this insight from Rabbi Steven Schwarzschild's "The Necessity of the Lone Man," in *Fellowship* (May, 1965), 16. Quoted in *The Non-Violent Cross*, 44.
84. Douglass, *Lightning East to West*, 21.

"Ask and it shall be given to you; search, and you will find; knock and the door will be opened to you." An experiment with truth, for Douglass, is the mode by which one discovers an inconceivable Reality. Again, he looks to the words of Jesus in Matthew 17:20–21 to show the power of experimenting with truth: "I tell you solemnly, if your faith were the size of a mustard seed you could say to this mountain, 'Move from here to there,' and it would move; nothing would be impossible for you."[85]

Douglass also looked to Gandhi as another "symbol and prophet of the kingdom of Reality." He understood Gandhi's nonviolent example as the model for experimentation with truth. "Gandhi's living definition of a non-violent revolution," says Douglass, "was that it was an experiment in truth."[86] Gandhi's life serves as an example of the possible, revealing the readiness of Reality to materialize through the practice of truth. "The revolutionary truth of Gandhi lies in what he became through his experiments," writes Douglass, "an objective force of truth and love. . . ."[87] Gandhi, like Jesus, also discloses the ego-renunciation and sacrifice inherent to an experiment with truth. From a law student in London to an Indian revolutionary, Gandhi endured a painful process of self-emptying to become the satyagrahi that he was. Again, Gandhi's Salt March stands as a perfect example of the sacrifice and self-emptying essential to truth experiments. Conceived of after long periods of difficult contemplation, the Salt March required a strong resistant witness to the untruth of British rule at the expense of political safety and physical comfort. Without employing violence, the March encouraged many to stand up for justice at the expense of their own lives. Yet Gandhi's experiments with truth extended far beyond the highly publicized events. He sought Truth with all of his being and knew the presence of God in his everyday acts of service. "The only feasible experiment with the truth of liberation," writes Douglass, "is Gandhi's experiment with truth, the kind of inquiry into the power and demands of truth which Gandhi undertook each day of his life with as much care as any lab technician ever took in treating explosive chemicals."[88]

Significantly, Douglass emphasizes that it is the revolution of the Kingdom itself which makes such experiments worthy. If I participate in serving the marginalized to placate my own sense of guilt, I am not ex-

---

85. Ibid., 21–22.
86. Douglass, *Resistance and Contemplation: The Way of Liberation*, 89.
87. Douglass, *Lightning East to West*, 21.
88. Douglass, *Resistance and Contemplation: The Way of Liberation*, 48.

perimenting with truth. The power of the Kingdom can only be realized to the extent that it is the center of my focus. Douglass explains, "The key to proceeding in those experiments is to realize radically that it is not so much our lives which count but rather whatever reality for change can enter the world through them."[89] As Jesus proclaims in Matthew 6:33, "strive first for the kingdom of God and his righteousness, and all these things will be given to you as well." The experiments with truth that constitute the revolution of the Kingdom ultimately point to the objective reality of the Kingdom, the focal point of Douglass's later writings. This objective Reality is what gives the cross its meaning, resistance its power, and contemplation its goal.

In his first book, we witness early on Douglass's criticism of Christianity for its seeming lack of faith in the objective power of God realized in truth. Very few Christians, he argues, have faith in Christianity's ability to change people by the power of truth. "A faith in truth's power to overcome the world by love and accepted suffering is as essential to an understanding of the Gospel as it is lacking in a Christianity which continues to endorse warfare."[90] Douglass's later works move beyond merely critiquing such unbelief to arguing forcefully for the objective reality and power of the Kingdom. His third book, *Lightning East to West,* is particularly adept at doing so. In this book, he clearly states his belief in "a loving, caring will at the center of reality which is as objective and concrete as a physical law. To experiment in its truth is to discover and confirm its reality."[91] Douglass compares this spiritual reality with the physical and psychic realities treated by Einstein and Jung, respectively. The law of spiritual change, he asserts, is as real as Einstein's laws of energy, and just as explosive. "I believe that there is, and there must be, a spiritual reality corresponding to $E=mc^2$," writes Douglass. "I believe that the human imperative of our end-time is that we discover the spiritual equation corresponding to Einstein's physical equation, and that then we begin to experiment."[92]

In addition, Douglass finds that Jung's analysis of synchronicity, or meaningful coincidence, reveals the reality of the oneness of God, humanity, and the universe, a oneness that we must have faith in so as to make present the Kingdom in the violence of our world. The experience of this

---

89. Douglass, *Lightning East to West*, 23.
90. Douglass, *The Non-Violent Cross*, 18.
91. Douglass, *Lightning East to West*, 2.
92. Ibid., 4–5.

oneness may be first realized in one's spiritual practice, but, as Douglass emphasizes, it must also be brought into the public sphere:

> The power of Reality to transform and unite us spiritually is seldom experienced even remotely because we seldom engage it . . . An experiment in reality is ultimately public. Such an experiment begins privately and personally, in the depths of prayer, consciousness, and the self—the first steps of metanoia and Jesus' reason for going out into the wilderness—*to see,* to see the possibility of a new Reality, perhaps inconceivable from his consciousness in Nazareth. But the new contemplative vision once realized requires practice and proclamation. The personal experiment in truth has to engage Reality ultimately in the community, and in the public order.[93]

Douglass further elaborates on how one engages the spiritual reality of the Kingdom in the world:

> The campaign can be seen as both spirit and body: Seeking first the kingdom of a deepening, widening community . . . in and through experiments of nonviolent direct action. Renouncing any fixation on the fruits of action . . . while trying to choose actions which in themselves carry the seeds of a moral and political crisis. Discovering life . . . through a faith willing to suffer.[94]

Douglass believes that to unite the inner experience of the Kingdom with the outer world of public life is to discover an explosive power, as real as when one brings together the polarities of the atom bomb. The supreme example of such explosive power is Jesus, who by going deeper into Reality through his death released the objective power of the Spirit. Indicating his reason for choosing the book title *Lightning East to West*, Douglass writes of the Kingdom's power: "The kingdom of Reality will be like lightning striking in the east and flashing far into the west when that hidden, latent energy of the unconscious Self which is God and humanity has been opened by sacrifice and allowed to surface into a conscious flash of truth, a force of oneness manifested in a spiritual chain reaction . . . ."[95]

As we have seen, Douglass's notion of revolution encompasses a number of elements which help to develop the importance of the Kingdom in his thought. The revolution of the Kingdom involves inner transformation through suffering, along with a renunciation of the fruits of action and technique. Both transformation and renunciation are embraced when one

93. Ibid., 14.
94. Ibid., 92.
95. Ibid., 37.

experiments in truth, placing absolute faith in the objective Reality of the Kingdom. Douglass summarizes his understanding of the revolution of the Kingdom in *Resistance and Contemplation*:

> The revolution is the kingdom among us realized by those who renounce the fruits, surrender to darkness and silence, and experience the suffering of the people and the power of the living God. The revolution is the kingdom conceived in contemplation and born into the world in resistance. The revolution is the kingdom of man liberated finally by the God already present in him.[96]

The Kingdom as the New Humanity of the End Times

Beyond understanding the notion of the kingdom as revolution, Douglass developed a theology of the kingdom as the new humanity revealed in Jesus Christ. Douglass believed that in the twentieth century, the critical conditions of the nuclear age both demanded and made increasingly possible the realization of this new humanity. In keeping with his sense of nuclear urgency, Douglass's discussion of the new humanity takes place within an eschatological context. Let us begin by briefly exploring Douglass's emphasis on the end times, followed by a concentrated examination of the new humanity in his theology.

As discussed earlier, Douglass reflected the concerns of his age, especially the alarm caused by the threat of nuclear destruction. Douglass himself was a self-proclaimed doomsdayer, believing that the nuclear age threatened to extinguish all of life on earth. In Lightning East to West, he provides the justification for his position, noting that a series of factors including famine, global terrorism, nuclear proliferation, and a general sense of increasing violence have initiated an all too real crisis in the modern world. We are brought to the brink. As Douglass writes, "In our own time, because of specific historical causes, we are living at the end of time."[97]

Accompanying these historical factors was a diminished sense of community in the West, as exemplified in its fascination with the individual self and consumerism. According to Douglass, the predominant focus on the self and security, with their outward manifestations of violence, have given rise to the nuclear end-time.[98]

---

96. Douglass, *Resistance and Contemplation: The Way of Liberation*, 108.
97. Douglass, *Lightning East to West*, 57.
98. Ibid., 59.

Douglass's notion of 'end times' is a far cry from the caricature of a supernatural apocalypticism. In his book *Lightning East to West,* he clarifies his understanding of the 'end times': It is the human *capacity* to end the world now, as can be done with 30 Trident missiles, now an actual possibility given the American arsenal of nuclear weapons. For Douglass, the end times have arrived, not because we will use the weapons at some future date, but simply because we have the capacity to do so in the present. The sheer ability to end all of life is a mark of our own spiritual and political depravity that is already contributing to the annihilation of the world. "For our generation," Douglass writes, "the symbol [of the end] has become a reality through the exploitation of millions of people, the rape of the earth, and a final judgment that will come from the spread of nuclear technology."[99]

Douglass's treatment of the eschaton serves as a response to what he considers the failure of contemporary Christian thought to confront the reality of the end time. Emphasizing the apocalyptic vision of Jesus, he decries the absence of a Christian alertness to the impending demise of humanity. The blame, he asserts, rests on Christian realism, which "has repressed the central reality of our end-time: the imminent destruction of all life on earth. It is a theology which has emphasized the reality of sin in history but has never faced squarely the emerging end of history through sin."[100]

Importantly, Douglass's emphasis on the eschatological nature of the nuclear age is not simply an expression of apocalyptic fervor, but serves to contrast this destructive possibility with the coming peaceable kingdom. Douglass attends to the end time in order to stress the critical importance of an ethic of nonviolent liberation, an ethic integral to the kingdom of God. Nothing less than this gospel of nonviolence will do, he urges, in order to reverse the rush of the world towards global destruction. Either we realize the Kingdom through a conversion to nonviolence, or we destroy ourselves. The Kingdom and the end of the world stand as the two divergent paths in the Nuclear Age. For Douglass, the choice between the two has, throughout history, never been clearer.[101] As he states, "The only realistic alternative to a doomsday vision inevitable from the history we know is the discovery of a power for human, global change...."[102]

The power for global change, however, will not be realized in the seeming power centers of politics, the military and the economy. The only

---

99. Douglass, *The Nonviolent Coming of God*, 3.
100. Douglass, *Lightning East to West*, 58.
101. Ibid., 17.
102. Ibid., 20.

real power for change lies with God. The choice between the kingdom and holocaust is therefore a spiritual one, intensified in the nuclear age. As Douglass writes, the Nuclear Age has become an Eschatological Age "in which man's power of global self-destruction has forced him into a confrontation with the depths of his spiritual self."[103] Either we realize our own emptiness in order to realize God's power, or we self-destruct.

In his fourth book, *The Nonviolent Coming of God,* Douglass develops further his apocalyptic thought by relating the contemporary nuclear situation to the *Sitz im Leben,* or 'life situation,' of Jesus. *The Nonviolent Coming of God* essentially articulates Jesus' alternative vision of the kingdom of God in light of his *Sitz im Leben* as a member of a colonized minority threatened with annihilation by the Roman imperial power. For Douglass, the threat of Jerusalem's destruction two thousand years ago correlates to our own situation today. Comparing the West's military agenda with that of Rome in Jesus' day, he writes, "Our security system needs low-intensity conflict and the threatened annihilation of cities to deter Third World peoples from revolution, just as Rome needed crucifixion and the threatened annihilation of cities to deter its provincial rebels."[104]

The impending destruction of Jerusalem could not have been insignificant to Jesus, asserts Douglass. On the contrary, it would have appeared as the end of the world to the Jewish people. The gospel message with its apocalyptic emphasis must therefore be considered in this context. In *The Nonviolent Coming of God,* Douglass centers his attention on Jesus' message and the end time as he would have experienced it. When one incorporates this context, one finds that Jesus' great revolution was the transformation of the end time into a new beginning for the world.

> The end of the world, for Jesus, was both a warning and the point of departure for his good news. . . . Jesus' prophecies are warnings of a terrible violence, to which he poses an alternative: the nonviolent kingdom of God, an upside-down kingdom whose first citizens are the poor and the starving (Luke 6:20–21).[105]

The thesis of *The Nonviolent Coming of God,* writes Douglass, is that, "far from announcing Jerusalem's destruction as inevitable, Jesus' whole public life was an effort to create a radically alternative Jewish society. . . .

---

103. Ibid., 5.
104. Douglass, *The Nonviolent Coming of God,* 14.
105. Ibid., 2–3.

His life, death, and resurrection were a transforming response to that *Sitz im Leben,* that life setting of total violence."[106]

Like all who bear the yoke of oppression, Jesus needed to formulate a response to his violent oppressors. Rather than respond with a militaristic revolution, Jesus chose to transform the violence of his oppressors through the acceptance of suffering on the cross. Yet his vision was not for the redemption of one violent act, but for the transformation of all violence and injustice. Douglass writes that Jesus' "response was a deepening vision of a nonviolent transformation of his people, in which the kingdom of God, and 'the Human Being,' became his principal terms for expressing a new reality."[107]

Jesus' vision of 'the Human Being' is a symbol of the transformation of the end time into a new beginning. Douglass draws the symbol of 'the Human Being' from a nuanced translation of Jesus' self-designation as 'Son of Man,' or in Aramaic, *Bar Enasha.* He employs Walter Wink's suggestion that it is better to translate *Bar Enasha* as the True Humanity, the Human Being, a divinely revolutionized humanity, or, as employed by Martin Luther King, Jr., 'Beloved Community.'[108] Douglass finds that it is helpful to see Jesus as the 'Human Being' in this collective and archetypal sense, as it connects Jesus' return with the nonviolent transformation of the world.

> The Human Being in Jesus' vision of transformation simply means Humanity, a divinely revolutionized Humanity. It is Humanity, a New Humanity transformed by God, which Jesus envisions as seated at the right hand of Power and coming with the clouds of heaven. This nonviolent coming of God in Jesus, in Israel, and in all of Humanity was Jesus' experience of God, an experience which spilled over from the symbol of the kingdom of God to the symbol of the Human Being, Humanity.[109]

Within his own experience as a human, Jesus recognized the rising revolution of God within humanity. Jesus knew that through his own nonviolent self-emptying, the kingdom itself could be incarnated in a new humanity. This, according to Douglass, is the Second Coming—the Son

---

106. Ibid., 15.

107. Ibid., 35.

108. Letter from Walter Wink to James Douglass, May 5, 1988. Quoted in Douglass, *The Nonviolent Coming of God,* 36.

109. Douglass, *The Nonviolent Coming of God,* 56.

of Man, or Human Being, transforming all humans through nonviolent love. As Douglass explains,

> It is this Second Coming of *Bar Enasha*, rolling across the world in the creation of a nonviolent humanity, that can be identified with the radically hopeful vision Jesus of Nazareth had for the Human Being, a collective Human Being, almost two thousand years ago. Jesus' vision of a nonviolent coming of God in *Bar Enasha*, which in the early church's understanding became Jesus' Second Coming in himself, is happening today.[110]

In his treatment of Jesus' Second Coming in a new humanity, Douglass criticizes the way many Christians deny the incarnation of Jesus in the present and his potential to transform the world from within us by conflating the nuclear holocaust with the Second Coming. These 'nuclear evangelists' as he refers to them, are "preachers of Jesus' return in judgment on a nuclear cloud. . . . The nuclear evangelists' Second Coming has in fact become so distorted and militarized a doctrine as to become indistinguishable from a Pentagon war scenario."[111] The problem, says Douglass, is that a misguided position such as nuclear evangelism does not allow for a new humanity made possible through Jesus, a humanity that has the power to free the world from injustice and violence. We are not saved so easily, writes Douglass, from the consequences of our choices. There is no reason to think that Christ's second coming should be any different than the first, which was a revolution of self-emptying poverty, not a powerful military coup.

Indeed, Douglass argues that we are involved in a constant struggle between violence and the second coming of Jesus in the new humanity. Understanding violence as dehumanization, Douglass believes God's way is the opposite of violence: humanization. The power of Christ's redemptive presence is only possible through the humanization of nonviolence. Just as there was no room for violence in Jesus' own life, there is no room for violence in the new humanity, which is, in essence, Jesus' return. As Douglass states, "The most fruitful question . . . in a second coming is not one of objective identity . . . but rather the more pointed question in ourselves of how a community might now live in most complete fidelity to the way of truth and love given in the first coming. . . ."[112]

Like the end of the world, Jesus' Second Coming is not out of time, limited to some future event, but fully in time and already occurring.

---

110. Ibid., 37.
111. Ibid., 38.
112. Douglass, *Lightning East to West*, 65.

Douglass uses the parable of the paralytic to articulate Jesus' coming in the transformation of humanity. As the *Bar Enasha*, Jesus has the authority to transform humanity, just as he transformed the paralytic. "The paralytic walks away because he has become a new human being. Transformed within and without, he is freed from paralysis. The source of his freedom to walk again is *Bar Enasha*, a new humanity with a forgiving, transforming power of God within it that Jesus extends to him and that he simultaneously discovers in himself."[113] Like the parable of the paralytic, Douglass finds numerous parables in the gospel that point to the kingdom as an already present divine transformation of humanity. Much of his book, *The Nonviolent Coming of God*, is dedicated to the exegesis of these parables and a probing of the kingdom that they reveal.

Although his later works, such as *The Nonviolent Coming of God*, concentrate on the kingdom, Douglass does not depart from his emphasis on suffering and the cross. Indeed, the cross is integral to Douglass's understanding of the new humanity. One must have the willingness to take on the cross in order to experience the transformation and resurrection of Christ. Taking his cue from Martin Buber, Douglass asserts that, at the time of Jesus, resurrection was thought by Jews to be a communal resurrection, experienced by the community as a whole.[114] After the experience of the cross, the community can realize their new humanity in the corporate resurrection of Jesus. Jesus desired to share the resurrection, urging that "If anyone wants to be a follower of mine, let that person renounce self, take up the cross, and follow me" (Mark 8:34).[115] Jesus sought to make all aware of the life-giving path to the new humanity.

> As Mark makes abundantly clear, the disciples were careful to follow the Human Being only at a distance, and at the critical moments, not at all. The clear implication of the gospel story is that Jesus wanted the disciples with him all the way, as a new humanity. Instead, he was crucified between two believers in violence; no one else in his own community would then walk the nonviolent way as far as the cross and enter with him into the new humanity.... Abandoned by his followers, alone before his judge, anticipating execution, Jesus still saw that total divine revolution coming from within Humanity. He knew that God would somehow make it

---

113. Douglass, *The Nonviolent Coming of God*, 41.

114. Ibid., 45. For this insight, Douglass looks to Buber's *Two Types of Faith* (New York: Macmillan, 1951), 100.

115. See Douglass, *The Nonviolent Coming of God*, 45.

happen, and he was determined to embody it by his own death. He did, and the nonviolent coming of God took over.[116]

The transformation of power in the kingdom of God remains strong in Douglass's vision of a new humanity. He continues to stress that the seemingly powerless of the world can have a stronger power: the power of the kingdom. This power, of course, will not be realized in the same way that one realizes military or economic power. "This is the meaning," writes Douglass, "of that bedrock text of the Jesus tradition, Luke 17:20–21: 'The kingdom of God is not coming with signs to be observed; nor will they say, "Lo, here it is!" or "There!" for behold, the kingdom of God is within your power [*entos humon*].'"[117] The power of the kingdom is both within and among us, a divine power that develops as we are transformed.

Although the kingdom of God may be at hand, it is also paradoxically not in our own hands. "A breaking in of the kingdom of God is nothing that we can reasonably expect, though we can hope for it. Jesus suggests that the kingdom's shattering breakthrough into our lives may in fact be nothing that we want."[118] While our actions may be fed by the power of the kingdom, we ourselves will not have control over their consequences. The power of God that breaks into our lives is a power *for*, not a power *over*. Whereas the latter implies a power of domination and, in Douglass's view, sin, the former consists of a power to serve, love, and build community according to the example of God who accepted powerlessness to redeem humanity. As Douglass writes, "To the revolutionary of the Kingdom, liberation will mean finally the disappearance of all power over men in the new reality of the human family's communion with the God of Love. The Gospel suggests that the way to realize that vision is to live it now in its fullness."[119]

One may perhaps find Douglass's concepts of the new humanity and the revolution of the Kingdom compelling, yet lacking in the muddy practicalities of a lived reality. Indeed, there is a tendency in Douglass's writings for his moving vision to get lost among abstractions. In his discussion of the new humanity, for example, one can be left wondering what the actual breakthrough of love into history looks like. While Douglass does frequently offer numerous examples from his own life and the lives of others to illustrate his arguments, he rarely gives the kind of practical

---

116. Douglass, *The Nonviolent Coming of God*, 45, 56.
117. Ibid., 106.
118. Ibid., 94.
119. Douglass, *Resistance and Contemplation: The Way of Liberation*, 43.

prescriptions a reader might desire. Although clearly not detailed ethical formulas, two descriptions of nonviolent action and transforming power provide a glimpse of what Douglass understands to be the actual living out of the new humanity. "Nonviolent action," he explains, "embodies in a beginning way what and who the Spirit of God is: at one with the poor and the suffering, resisting injustice, loving enemies, and forgiving unforgivable actions. So when we act in that way . . . we begin to give God an opening into the world. God uses those openings in ways at which we can only marvel."[120] Again, Douglass gives a still somewhat abstract, but more diverse depiction of the loving and transforming power in the new humanity. Such power involves "loving enemies, forgiving debtors, recognizing outcasts as God's chosen ones, discovering truth in the opponent, seeking the infinite presence of God in our own fallible community."[121] Forgiveness, love, and solidarity, while open for interpretation, remain the mainstay of Douglass's understanding of the nonviolent kingdom.

The living and historical exemplars of nonviolence perhaps provide the strongest indication of how Douglass concretely understood the kingdom and the new humanity. These men and women were practitioners of nonviolent resistance who, in their stand against violence and injustice, were saying, "From now on you will see Humanity seated at the right hand of Power and coming on the clouds of heaven."[122] Douglass gives his readers a variety of exemplary people, from those who stand as cultural, religious, and political icons to those whose sacrifices often remain forgotten. Loreta Asanaviciute, for example, defended media centers in her recently independent Lithuanian republic. She gave her life in resistance when she was rolled over by a Soviet tank. Jo Ann Robinson demonstrated the truth of liberation by working diligently to spread the word regarding the Montgomery bus boycott, while Wang Weilin stood before the column of tanks in Tianenmen Square. Elsewhere Douglass looks to Dorothy Day, Mahatma Gandhi, Oscar Romero, the Berrigans, and Danilo Dolci whose profound and selfless acts of resistance proclaim the revolution and new humanity. The resistance of Martin Luther King, Jr. is also exemplary. The day before his death, King revealed a glimpse of the kingdom that particularly resonates with Douglass's understanding of the kingdom:

> It is no longer a choice between violence and nonviolence in this world; it's nonviolence or nonexistence. . . . We've got some dif-

---

120. Douglass, *The Nonviolent Coming of God*, 23.
121. Ibid., 113.
122. Ibid., 57.

ficult days ahead. But it doesn't matter with me now. Because I've been up to the mountaintop. And I don't mind. Like anybody, I would like to live a long life. Longevity has its place. But I'm not concerned about that now. I just want to do God's will. And [God's] allowed me to go up to the mountain. And I've looked over. And I've seen the promised land. I may not get there with you. But I want you to know tonight, that we, as a people will get to the promised land. And I'm happy, tonight. I'm not worried about anything. I'm not fearing any man. Mine eyes have seen the glory of the coming of the Lord.[123]

With these figures before us, it is not difficult for us, like King, to see the glory of the coming of the Lord. Faced with the lives and deaths of contemporaries such as Romero, Day, and King, the reader sees Douglass's new humanity and revolution less as a lofty ideology than a vivid reality, with very real implications.

Throughout this chapter we have been considering the Cross and the Kingdom as the two central themes in Douglass's treatment of nonviolence. These two themes must not be seen as distinct for they are everywhere intertwined in Douglass's thought. What they both point to, and what grounds nearly all of Douglass's prophetic intuitions, is what may be considered an ontology of nonviolence. The Cross and Kingdom equally participate in this realm of nonviolent communion. Beyond, or perhaps behind, the appearances of the world lies a truth grounded in God's own being, a truth that calls into question all violent pretensions to power. This ontology of nonviolence remains generally hidden, yet may be revealed in acts of contemplative resistance and nonviolent engagement, prolongations of the incarnation and tokens of God's breakthrough into history. This existential reality is the site that unifies Douglass's emphasis on both contemplation and resistance. The ontology of nonviolence calls forth a contemplation that also participates in its reality and therefore ushers in Christ-like acts of renunciation and resistance. Thus, it is to Douglass's ontology of nonviolence and the twin themes of contemplation and resistance that we now turn.

---

123. Martin Luther King, Jr. "I See the Promised Land," in *A Testament of Hope: The Essential Writings of Martin Luther King, Jr.*, ed. James M. Washington (San Francisco: Harper & Row, 1986), 280, 286. Quoted in Douglass, *The Nonviolent Coming of God*, 34.

4

An Ontology of Nonviolence
The Uniting of Contemplation and Resistance

THE PREVIOUS three chapters have provided the necessary background to a more concentrated consideration of James Douglass's main project. Moving in concentric circles, we began by examining the general environment that formed Douglass's life and thought before circling closer to consider the more explicit influences on Douglass's life. As we advanced to consider Douglass's work itself, it was necessary to explicate the general themes that thread throughout his writings, themes such as the cross and the kingdom. Now we find ourselves poised to analyze the central intuition animating Douglass's project, a vision which I identify as an ontology of nonviolence. In order to examine his vision, this chapter will consist of two parts. First we will consider explicitly the ontology of nonviolence as the project driving Douglass's work. Secondly, we will explicate the integral role of contemplative spirituality in this project. In doing so, we will witness precisely how Douglass integrates a contemplative spirituality with political and social involvement in his understanding of nonviolence.

An Ontology of Nonviolence

While Douglass does not explicitly claim to create an ontology of nonviolence, the concept is suggested implicitly throughout his works. Moreover, it is my contention that the concept of ontological nonviolence, though rarely treated categorically in these works, forms a background presupposition which lends life and depth to all of Douglass's reflections. This nonviolent theology is the underlying premise which shapes his thought and drives his prophetic voice. But what is this ontology of nonviolence? In order to help our investigation, I offer a preliminary definition in the following paragraph before considering the way Douglass employed the phrase as drawn from Thomas Merton.

Briefly, an ontology of nonviolence connotes a nonviolent Reality in which one participates through acts of nonviolence. For Douglass, this entails viewing reality as fundamentally constituted by a relationship to the divine. Being itself is given in an act of divine generosity that constitutes creation. Unlike the Nietzschean will to power, Douglass's ontology is a non-competitive ontology of love. Douglass sees the way that the constitution of reality (ontology) necessarily issues forth in performative and existential responses. Because reality is at its base relational and nonviolent, it elicits, from our deepest and most authentic selves, nonviolent ways of inhabiting the world. As an ontological reality, nonviolence is neither a tactic for achieving desired ends nor a prohibition of violent behavior. It is, rather, a comportment to the 'grain of the universe,'[1] a manner of being that engages with God through its adherence to Truth and Love.

For clarification, it is helpful to consult Thomas Merton's application of the term 'ontology of nonviolence,' and its treatment by Douglass. In the essay entitled "Thomas Merton's Glimpse of the Kingdom," Douglass looks to Merton for insight on how one can transform a world of overwhelming violence. He references the last paragraphs of Merton's book, *Mystics and Zen Masters,* where Merton questions "the Western acceptance of a 'will to transform others' in terms of one's own prophetic insight accepted as a norm of pure justice." Merton continues:

> Is there not an 'optical illusion' in an eschatological spirit which, however much it may appeal to *agape*, seeks only to transform persons and social structures *from the outside?* Here we arrive at a basic principle, one might almost say an ontology of nonviolence, which requires further investigation.[2]

Commenting on Merton's insight, Douglass writes:

> Perhaps it was that further investigation into an ontology of nonviolence which Merton was engaged in when he died in Bangkok in 1968. Can we join now in such an investigation ourselves? What was Merton pointing to as that basic principle, or ontology of nonviolence, which would go beyond a 'transformation from the outside' and beyond 'one's own prophetic insight accepted

---

1. Stanley Hauerwas, *With the Grain of the Universe: The Church's Witness and Natural Theology: Being Gifford Lectures Delivered at the University of St. Andrews in 2001* (Grand Rapids, MI: Brazos Press, 2001).

2 Thomas Merton, *Mystics and Zen Masters*, 287–88. Cited in James Douglass, "Thomas Merton's Glimpse of the Kingdom," 205. The significance of this passage for Douglass can be seen in its repeated use in a number of his works. Aside from "Thomas Merton's Glimpse of the Kingdom" (1981), it also appears in *Resistance and Contemplation* (1972), 58; "Non-violence and Metanoia" (1974), 31; *Lightning East to West* (1983), 13; and "Civil Disobedience as Prayer" (1996), 25.

An Ontology of Nonviolence

as a norm of pure justice'? Is there a genuine transformation of the world possible beyond the 'optical illusion' of our 'outside' struggles? Can we perhaps understand our optical illusion critically enough to open our lives to the reality beyond it?[3]

For both Thomas Merton and James Douglass, an ontology of nonviolence indicates the possibility for social and political transformation apart from efforts to impose external change. Nonviolence itself is rooted in an internal state of being which shares in the nonviolent essence of all being, or God. As such, acts of nonviolence involve an inner transformation from which emerges a power for the transformation of others.

In his works, Douglass answers an emphatic "Yes!" to his own question regarding the possibility of a real transformation of the world, outside of our own misdirected attempts at such. Three decades of writing all attend to this endeavor: a critical understanding of our "optical illusion" and an opening of our lives to the nonviolent reality beyond it. Indeed, Douglass had long considered nonviolence to be more than simply the transformation of the world from the 'outside.' As witnessed in his early writings onward, he integrated suffering love into his understanding of nonviolence as a sacramental participation in the suffering love of Christ. From the start, Gandhi played a key role in Douglass's interpretation of nonviolence as a force of truth, worthy in its own right, apart from its ability to effect political change. From Gandhi, Douglass learned that nonviolence was not a tactic whereby a more just world could be created from the imaginations and utopian dreams of confident revolutionaries. On the contrary, nonviolence was a way of being. It did not merely involve laboring to build a more loving and just society, but required that one be loving and just at the center of oneself.

As revealed in Douglass's writings, nonviolence is not realized merely in action but in one's nature, as one conforms one's own being to the ultimate Being through *metanoia*, or a conversion of heart and soul. By doing so, one essentially becomes the Truth and Love of God, and brings such Love into the world, transforming it from within. Beyond a simplistic understanding of pacifism, which merely refuses to commit violence because of ethical prescriptions, Douglass's nonviolence is an active love that brings a person into communion with God. To better elucidate Douglass's ontology of nonviolence, let us consider again the themes of the Kingdom and the Cross which we explored in the previous chapter.

---

3. Douglass, "Thomas Merton's Glimpse of the Kingdom," 205.

A Question of Being

The Kingdom and the Cross

Douglass's kingdom theology is an important part of his nonviolent ontology. Nonviolence has sometimes been conceived in eschatological terms; that is, as a way of living in accord with the expectation of a coming kingdom. In this view, nonviolent practice is justified in the eschatological unveiling of God's reign. If we conceive of Douglass's nonviolence in eschatological terms—a conception warranted by Douglass's own apocalyptic language—then we must say that his is a realized eschatology. According to Douglass, we participate in the kingdom through our nonviolent being. Borrowing the term from Gandhi, Douglass's "experiments in truth" attest to this participation in Being, through which the kingdom breaks into history. Fundamental to this point is Douglass's emphasis on a "permanent ontological relationship between God and man in truth."[4] He writes of this ontological relationship revealed by both Gandhi and Pope John XXIII in *The Non-Violent Cross*, and although he mentions it only explicitly in this one instance, all of his works attest to this ontology of truth.

As we have seen, renouncing the fruits of one's actions is inherent to an experiment in truth whereby we open ourselves to God's power. By renouncing fruits, we are able to focus on nonviolent action itself as an ontological reality. To be concerned with effective results, on the other hand, is to attempt in Merton's words to transform the world from the outside. An ontology of nonviolence does not change the world from the outside, through effective technique, but from the inside, by participation in the divine Truth and the realization of the kingdom on earth.

The cross, too, is integral to Douglass's understanding of nonviolence as an ontological reality. As we have seen, nonviolence, for Douglass, is the suffering love that 'opens our lives' to the present reality of the kingdom. The cross is united with the reality of the kingdom, not through cause and effect, but because of the divine presence inherent in sacrificial love. Douglass's understanding of the cross emphasizes the ontological nature of nonviolence: self-emptying opens one to act with nonviolence, and suffering is the practice of nonviolent love.

I have argued that the cross and the kingdom, the key themes of Douglass's major works, help to explain his implied ontology of nonviolence. In order to clarify this vision further, it will be beneficial to look at the way Douglass also engages the question of 'outside' versus 'inside' transformation. Although this is not one of his major themes, it does appear significantly in a key article, "Thomas Merton's Glimpse of the

---

4. Douglass, *The Non-Violent Cross*, 90.

Kingdom." Therefore, in order to continue our exploration of Douglass's latent ontology of nonviolence, let us turn to consider the themes of this article in the following section.

Ontology of Nonviolence: Transformation from the Inside

In exploring the context of Douglass's life and thought, we witnessed his struggle with technological society, and its tendency towards efficient management and dehumanization. Likewise, we noted his severe critique of milieu-Catholicism and its failure to recognize the humanity of the suffering Jesus and the deeply personal commitment required of faith. These systems and structures with which Douglass struggled—nuclear technology, military agendas, the oppression of the poor, and a Church of stability, security and complacency—all focus primarily on the protection of a "false self" through control and coercion. Their emphasis is less on the interiority of being and authentic human relationships than on external control for the sake of the ego.

Douglass was in line with the reforming currents of his day, which saw a return to conscience, "the real," and the subjective over the technological and bureaucratic. His theology of nonviolence reflects this movement toward interiority. In his essay, "Thomas Merton's Glimpse of the Kingdom," Douglass seeks to articulate an ontology of nonviolence by emphasizing transformation from the 'inside.' He clarifies the difference between 'outside' and 'inside' transformation of the world when he writes that "those few who have perceived reality from its very center . . . must have something to say about our activist struggle to move the mountain of the world from the surface."[5] The struggle to transform the world, he writes, is, in fact, an illusion. This illusion of struggle is born out of the ignorance of the ego. Douglass writes:

> [This is the ego] in each of us which would like to regard itself as an identity separate from the world, as a separate identity which stands over and against the objective mountain of suffering and injustice. But 'as you are, so is the world.' The mountain of the world with its overwhelming evil and suffering is not out there. In a very deep sense, that mountain is in here. The world in its deepest evil is, in fact, me.[6]

---

5. Douglass, "Thomas Merton's Glimpse of the Kingdom," 205.
6. Ibid., 206.

This emphasis is fundamental to Douglass's ontology: As we are, so is the world. To embrace nonviolence is not to change the world apart from ourselves; it is to change the world through ourselves. Douglass explains, "As we are, so is the world because the world derives its fundamental shape and definitions from ourselves, and primarily from our ego . . . . As we are, so is the world, in so deep-rooted a sense that the world can and will be transformed only and exactly to the extent that I undergo transformation in myself."[7]

Nonviolence transforms the world from the inside because, by Douglass's definition, it is Love and Truth lived in reality. Contrary to 'outside' transformation which is often willing to compromise truth and love in order to effect change, the ultimate goal of nonviolence is simply to unite with Truth and embody Love. Douglass gives concrete examples from his own experiences of resistance that testify to the priority of human relationships in the ontology of nonviolence. In *Lightning East to West,* he recounts the interactions of the protestors and the workers on the Trident missile base in Bangor, Washington. Respecting the workers and the police was necessary to fulfill the purpose of the resistance, which was "not to stop the Trident submarine and missile system," but instead to "change ourselves."[8] It is vital for Douglass that in resisting structural evil, one recognizes the shared humanity, and shared *complicity* with those who are directly involved in perpetuating the evil. Only then can transformation truly occur, as a communal *metanoia* realized in the oneness of humanity. Nonviolence as an ontology exists in relationships, and attention must therefore be directed to these: "Our hope should not be for any strategic victories over such representatives of the state, but rather loving, nonviolent relationships with them in the midst of our arrests, trials, and prison sentences."[9]

As we have seen, Douglass's ontology of nonviolence emphasizes change from within. Recognizing our shared complicity in the world's evils serves as the starting point for change, for 'As we are, so is the world.' Douglass articulates this inner dimension of political change in his article on civil disobedience: "Protesting against something for which we ourselves are profoundly responsible is a futile exercise in hypocrisy. The evil of nuclear war is not external to us, so that it can be isolated in the state or in the Nuclear Train loaded with hydrogen bombs. The nature of the evil

---

7. Ibid., 207.
8. Douglass, *Lightning East to West*, 79.
9. James Douglass, "Civil Disobedience as Prayer," in *Swords into Plowshares: Nonviolent Direct Action for Disarmament, Peace, Social Justice*, ed. Arthur J. Laffin and Anne Montgomery (Marion, SD: Fortkamp Publishing, 1996), 25.

lies in our cooperation with it."[10] According to Douglass, when we try to end our cooperation with evil in one way, it often happens that we "begin cooperating with it more intensely and blindly in another way, defining the evil in a way external to us that only deepens and hardens its actual presence in ourselves."[11] To bring world change, then, we must begin by accepting fully the evil within ourselves and, in deep humility, turn towards God in faith. Thus, to participate in the ontology of nonviolence, we have to participate from within the depths of our own being.

Having shown how personal transformation is at the center of Douglass's nonviolent ontology, we must revisit the fundamental role of contemplative spirituality in this ontology. Indeed, contemplation exists, for Douglass, as an inseparable aspect of nonviolence, an aspect all too often neglected among those who wish to change the world from the 'outside.' After his experience in the late sixties with the disillusionment of his generation, and fed by study of Merton, Douglass sought to develop further the concept of nonviolence as an inner reality, or way of being, informed by a spiritual posture. Recognizing the significance of inner transformation to Douglass's ontology of nonviolence, we turn our attention to his notion of contemplation as the primary means of such transformation.

Contemplation in the Ontology of Nonviolence

By now, we should be able to see the way that Douglass's peaceable theology is mirrored in his ontology of nonviolence. The nonviolence of God issues in a creation whose foundations are similarly irenic. Because reality is fundamentally peaceable, we become peacemakers ourselves not through an exertion of effort but through a path of abandonment. This brings us to the central role of contemplation in Douglass's thought. Contemplation is the means by which human beings live in harmony with the nonviolence of both God and creation. It exists for Douglass as one of the primary ways we adopt the spiritual posture of self-emptying which results in our transformation. Contemplation is an effortless-effort that opens us to the divine and allows God's nonviolence to become the substance of our own lives. It is the way that humans enter into the *metonoia* discussed previously and the transformation that necessarily follows. In this section we will begin by unearthing Douglass's definition of contemplation, which will allow us to ascertain how contemplative activity is woven into the fabric

10. Ibid., 27.
11. Ibid.

of the real (i.e., the ontology of nonviolence). For Douglass, contemplation is the recognition of our fundamental poverty, a poverty of the self. Recognizing this poverty, as we will show in the subsequent section, opens a space for the human to encounter God and to become transformed, to allow the kingdom to come on earth. But let us first attend to Douglass's definition.

Characteristically, Douglass never defines contemplation systematically. However, the term is prevalent enough in his works that one may obtain a clear understanding of its rich, while imprecise, meaning. Douglass defines contemplation most explicitly in *Resistance and Contemplation*, when he writes, "To contemplate is to look intently at reality, and to begin to see it as it is."[12] Contemplation begins with an acknowledgment of a transcendent, yet present reality, which exposes the illusions created by human autonomy. To see this reality clearly, one must interact with it through contemplation. For Douglass, however, contemplation goes much deeper than generic prayer. One does not, for example, assert one's own will in dialogue with the divine. Rather, one opens oneself to the love of God and the truth of one's own poverty, insecurities, and illusions.

Contemplation as Poverty and Self-Emptying

The concept of inner poverty is vital to Douglass's understanding of contemplation. In contemplation, we voluntarily expose ourselves to the painful knowledge of both our profound emptiness and the many ways we have tried to mask this with our "false selves." Indeed, the recognition of the poverty of the autonomous self is inherent to an unobstructed view of reality. Douglass articulates this in reference to his own generation's need for spiritual grounding. "Contemplation," he writes, "begins with a sharp perception of our rock-bottom poverty and powerlessness—not so much in the sense of leaders assassinated and campaigns destroyed, the preliminaries to a deeper onslaught, as in the sense of an individual self exposed finally without props and pretensions." Without such contemplation, resisting unjust structures through civil disobedience,

> can be done in a way that, while it is apparently not cooperating with nuclear war, still ends up cooperating with an illusion that underlies nuclear war. In any attitude of resistance to the state there is a kind of demonic underside, a power turned upside down

---

12. Douglass, *Resistance and Contemplation: The Way of Liberation*, 51.

that wishes to gain the upper hand. Civil disobedience that is not done as prayer is especially vulnerable to its underside.[13]

On the other hand, resistance undertaken with a contemplative posture does not grasp for power or self-fulfillment. Rather, contemplation provides an awareness of one's own poverty that allows for a relinquishment of an often violent protection of the ego. Contemplation, Douglass writes, occurs when "each of us is left alone to face himself."[14]

The renunciation of the self, according to Douglass, is the most significant way of recognizing one's poverty and facing oneself alone. Only through self-emptying can we contemplate Reality in its fullest. The self that must be faced is that self that clings to security and contentment, and is willing to commit violence in order to do so. This is the false self articulated by Merton, a violent self that relies on illusions to protect the emptiness at the center of one's life.[15] As Douglass writes: "At its center contemplation is receptivity to the wind of the Spirit, but is conditioned by my active resistance to the fears and claims of the self: claims of comfort, security, self-control."[16] This resistance to the claims of the self involves a renunciation of self-interest—the peeling away of self-righteousness and self-justification. Even further, it involves the recognition that one is alone, powerless, and impotent to solve the problems of the world. As Douglass writes, "The prophet is therefore engaged in a double struggle: to respond with all his power to those whose suffering becomes his own, and at the same time to accept his personal and human limits which are based on a radical poverty of being."[17]

To enter into the silence and solitude of contemplation, one must renounce the security of pretensions that create the illusion of a strong, empowered self. As a consequence, we are each left alone to face ourselves in our own poverty—entering into a dark night of the soul and of the world.[18] We are stripped of the will to transform others. We recognize our limits and face ourselves in the desert without superficial political or social supports. Through hopelessness and despair we are stripped of our faith in

---

13. Douglass, "Civil Disobedience as Prayer," 24.
14. Douglass, *Resistance and Contemplation: The Way of Liberation*, 51.
15. Douglass most thoroughly elucidates the self that is to be renounced, incorporating Merton's notion of the false self, in "Civil Disobedience as Prayer," 26–27.
16. Douglass, *Resistance and Contemplation: The Way of Liberation*, 69.
17. Ibid., 144.
18. Ibid., 185.

direct action and specific causes. Contemplation of God, and therefore of our own poverty, is as a disciplined loss of self-control.

In referring to the kenotic nature of the contemplative posture, Douglass employs words such as darkness, silence, and receptivity. Silence is an important element of his personal experience of contemplation: "I knew the Way as giving itself in the deepest silence . . . . I learned to walk in the Way by letting go of the thinking kind of listening . . . and letting silence enter."[19] For Douglass, nonviolent contemplation requires that we accept the emptiness and illusion of the autonomous self in order to embrace God's will rather than our own—a will that calls us to suffering love.

One cannot investigate Douglass's understanding of contemplation without acknowledging the influence of the Eastern religious traditions of Taoism and Zen Buddhism.[20] Douglass himself asserts, "It is to the East, and to Zen in particular, that Western contemplatives today look increasingly for guidance."[21] Looking to the Tao, with its contrast of yin and yang, he enriches his own contrast of contemplation and active resistance. Douglass interprets the yin as contemplation, "receptive, yielding, life-giving water, the cloud, the dark slope of the mountain." This is set in contrast to the yang of resistance which is "active, firm, the power of command, the banner waving in the sun, the bright side of the mountain."[22] Zen, too, enhances the idea of contemplation for Douglass. He equates contemplation with Satori, or awakening, which he describes as "the acquiring of an absolutely new point of view toward life and the world, or an intuitive looking into the nature or suchness of things, as opposed to a verbal or analytic understanding of them."[23] The contemplation of Zen enlightens the possibilities of Christian contemplation:

> By liberating man from a restrictive ego, Zen allows him to open his eyes and see. What he sees is a void which is infinite. What he sees is the suchness of things. What he sees is indescribably one.

---

19. Douglass, "Prison," 52.

20. Douglass uses D. T. Suzuki's introduction to *The Texts of Taoism*, translated by James Legge (New York: The Julian Press, 1959) as well as Hellmut Wilhelm's *Change: Eight Lectures on the I Ching* (New York: Harper Torchbooks, 1964) for some of his interpretation of the Tao, or Way. His reference to Zen is primarily based on D.T. Suzuki's work *Essays in Zen Buddhism,* First Series (New York: Grove Press, 1961) and Merton's own writings on the subject including *Zen and the Birds of Appetite* (1968) and *Mystics and Zen Masters* (1967).

21. Douglass, *Resistance and Contemplation: The Way of Liberation*, 54.

22. Ibid., 67.

23. Ibid., 60.

And that may in fact have been what Jesus saw in a pure perception of being, although both Merton and Suzuki agree that Jesus added a dimension of faith to the contemplation of reality which characterizes Zen. The perception of Zen is an instantaneous, living insight into being, so that we look at things as they are and so that we live now, on the ground where we are standing.[24]

Contemplation, as learned from Zen, is an unmitigated perception of being. In the Christian context, this being is God, realized in the "inner unity of silent prayer."[25]

Just how exactly such contemplation is practiced remains unexplored in Douglass's writings, as does a categorical analysis of reality, unity, and being. Neither a metaphysician nor spiritual cartographer, Douglass is restricted to the abstract terminology of the prophet. As one must do with many mystics and spiritual writers whose experiences of the divine elude language, Douglass's reader must settle for aesthetic and metaphorical descriptions of his primary concepts rather than systematic definitions. One witnesses this in his use of mystical language with regard to the self-emptying nature of contemplation:

> Below the measurable fragments which claim exclusive reality in our eyes, below the daylight self which assumes *I* am in control, below the radical poverty which itself descends a ladder from dark night into darker morning, below all images and below all darkness, in the pit of a spiritual void lies the mystery of being and its unity.[26]

While the method of contemplative praxis evades the reader, it is clear that, for Douglass, the spirituality of nonviolence is one of descent. The contemplative component of nonviolence is a descent into the void and the darkness, into a renounced, emptied, and poor self. Like the church of the 1960s, Douglass sees the movement of faith as a movement downward into reality, an engagement with the world rather than withdrawal. Douglass's is an embrace of human fragility, an encounter with the Incarnation, and, in an acceptance of the void, unity with God.

Contemplation in an Ontology of Nonviolence

As we have seen thus far, Douglass's understands contemplation as a posture of silent, self-emptying prayer which allows one to perceive the unity

---

24. James Douglass, "Resistance, Contemplation, Liberation," *Katallagete*, Spring (1971): 17.

25. Douglass, "Non-Violence and Metanoia," 29.

26. Douglass, *Resistance and Contemplation: The Way of Liberation*, 146.

and essence of being. With this understanding, one is able to ascertain the relevance of contemplation for an ontology of nonviolence. According to Douglass, contemplation that surrenders the self to the truth, love, and unity of God, and consequently faces its own emptiness, necessarily involves metanoia, or the turning of one's heart and soul towards the divine. The type of contemplation, writes Douglass, that results in metanoia, will wrench me "away from my household idols to confront the living God."[27] In the process of uniting with God's nonviolent being, one becomes nonviolent as well. Selfless and sacrificial love indwells one's being, not only prohibiting violent behavior but pushing such a person to act justly and lovingly towards others at any cost. No longer a choice, this inner compulsion also provides strength for the endurance of suffering in love. This is the reason Douglass believes that contemplation provides the rock on which to stand when resisting the dehumanization of the world. Without it, resistance becomes overwhelmed by one's own sense of powerlessness in the face of the world's injustice.

As previously discussed, relationships are vital to an ontology of nonviolence. To develop such nonviolent relationships, one must embrace a contemplative posture in order to access selfless love. As Douglass writes, contemplative resistance, or

> civil disobedience as prayer is not an act of defiance but an act of obedience to a deeper, interior will within us and within the world that is capable of transforming the world. 'Thy kingdom come, thy will be done.' To live out the kingdom of God through such an action is to live in a loving relationship to our brothers and sisters in the police force, in courts, and in jails, recognizing God's presence in each of us.[28]

The role of self-emptying contemplation in an ontology of nonviolence is perhaps best elucidated in "Thomas Merton's Glimpse of the Kingdom," as Douglass looks to Merton's "ultimate experience of Reality" for insight into how one realizes ontological nonviolence. Merton, in contemplating the stone Buddhas at Polonnaruwa only one week before his death, wrote that "All problems are resolved and everything is clear, simply because what matters is clear . . . everything is emptiness and everything is compassion."[29] Douglass comments:

27. Ibid., 59.
28. Douglass, "Civil Disobedience as Prayer," 28.
29. Thomas Merton, *The Asian Journal of Thomas Merton*, ed. Patrick Hart Naomi Burton, and James Laughlin (New York: New Directions Publishing, 1973). Cited in

> In our resistance to humankind's destruction, we need to live and act in that spirit of ultimate emptiness and compassion if we are to experience transformation. . . . I believe that Thomas Merton's ultimate experience of Reality, and the insight emerging from it, is the foundation we need for nonviolent direct action—that 'ontology of nonviolence' for action that will transform our nuclear end-time into the kingdom of God.[30]

Douglass finds this incident to be a prime example of the exigency of contemplation for an ontology of nonviolence. As exemplified in Merton's life, contemplation is integral to nonviolence as the opening to nonviolent divine truth and love which transforms people and their subsequent actions. Contemplation is necessary for a nonviolent ontology's 'transformation from the inside.' It is not the psychological experience of a private subject but an event of transformative communion with the deepest springs of reality. In this sense, contemplation is eminently public; it unites us with that "hidden ground of love," as Merton called it, that is the wellspring of all creation and therefore moves beyond the private illusions and fantastic projections of the false self.

It is helpful here to remember what Douglass means when he speaks of the self that must be emptied. The self from which we must seek freedom is the self enslaved to structures of economic, political, social and racial oppression. It is the self that exists under the burden of the modern technocratic world. In recognizing the poverty of this false self, the self controlled and constructed by technocrats and market demagogues, we are set free and brought into alignment with the nonviolent structure of the world. We are transformed from within, not by the exertion of our own wills, and not by the will to power of hostile forces, but by the love of God who creates the world in peace.

Because it is lived, contemplation is also political, thus establishing the connection between resistance and contemplation. Contemplative silence is not a withdrawal but an engagement with reality at its most robust, most involved, most concrete. This ontology of nonviolence is why, as the very manner of Douglass's life seems to insist, *contemplation is political.* For the Christian initiated into the original peace of Christ's kingdom there is no question of personal piety versus public service. The two are correlative. A spirituality of self-emptying deeply effects how we involve ourselves with the structures of the world which attempt to buttress our false selves. A spirituality that recognizes its own poverty for the sake of welcoming the

Douglass, "Thomas Merton's Glimpse of the Kingdom," 209.

30. Douglass, "Thomas Merton's Glimpse of the Kingdom," 209–10.

love of God cannot help but resist the world's systems of dehumanization. As Douglass articulates it most clearly, "man becomes God by renouncing power and becoming nothing . . . and for a few hours man is transfigured on the cross and resists with the power of God: The world changes."[31] As Douglass laid it out clearly across one of his titles: civil disobedience is prayer. For this reason, contemplation and resistance may be differentiated but never divided.

---

31. Douglass, *Resistance and Contemplation: The Way of Liberation*, 77.

5

Conclusion
Constructive Engagements with James Douglass's Theology of Nonviolence

WHERE HAVE we come from, and where do we go from here? Before we can begin to examine the relevance of Douglass's nonviolent theology for today, let us first give a concise review of how we have arrived at this point, briefly tracing the movements of this book and articulating again Douglass's central vision. We will then be poised to undertake a critical engagement with Douglass's work, raising three primary areas of concern: dualism, abstraction, and the focus on suffering. Following this, we will be able to discern just what significance an ontology of nonviolence may hold for us now, nearly forty years after Douglass published his first book.

The writings of James Douglass integrate in text and in theory what Douglass has also united in his life and witness: contemplation and resistance. Through a careful reading of Douglass's works, we have sought to understand how these often disparate movements can be brought together. In order to do this, we began with a thorough consideration of the historical surroundings and influential people that contributed to the evolution of Douglass's thought. We saw how American culture in the middle of the twentieth century, with its nuclear apocalypticism and growing critique of institutions, helped to spur Douglass's passionate interest in the need for resistance—resistance, based on a gospel imperative, to the forces of domination, inequity, and dehumanization.

We then saw how the circumstances surrounding the demise of the peace movement helped Douglass to recognize that resistance to injustice and violence cannot be autonomously sustained. Douglass discovered in contemplation a more radical species of resistance, and developed his theology of nonviolence in response. In this, Douglass was not alone and he learned from both his predecessors and his peers. It was important then, for our understanding of Douglass to be buttressed by a consideration of some of these influences on him and so we examined the figures of

Dorothy Day, Mahatma Gandhi, and Thomas Merton, paying special attention to what Douglass learned from each.

From history and the influence of others, we turned to Douglass's theology and paid close attention to Douglass's central themes of the Cross and the Kingdom. In considering these themes, I argued that Douglass's theology spills over into a unifying concept of an ontology of nonviolence, a vision of a nonviolent reality at the base of all things in which we participate. This ontology, in turn, is integrally related to Douglass's conception of contemplation, the self-emptying that allows the non-violent Kingdom to manifest through the very roots of our being. Through this discussion of contemplation in Douglass's ontology of nonviolence, we were able to see more clearly the way he unites contemplation and resistance—two vital movements of self-emptying which together realize the Kingdom of God.

Douglass's ability to unite contemplative spirituality and active resistance to unjust structures is one of the great contributions of his ontology of nonviolence. Recognizing the value of Douglass's ontology, however, does not mean that we can overlook the difficulties that emerge in his works. In the pages that follow, I will offer a critique of Douglass's works based on his own central intuitions. Such a critique is not intended to discredit his theology by any means, but rather to raise questions that, with further treatment, can strengthen the argument for an ontology of nonviolence. Across the spectrum of Douglass's writings, I find three areas that fall short of his vision's potential. By indulging too often in dualism, resting in abstractions, and embracing an ethic of suffering with little qualification, Douglass at times abandons his own best intuitions and complicates the reception that his works should generate in practice.

The Problem of Dualism

Douglass's greatest weakness, perhaps, is his tendency to see the world dualistically. This is not a great surprise, as the formative period of his thought, the 1950s, tended toward dualism in its pitting of 'good' capitalism against the 'evil' of communism. Interestingly, Douglass's project is one of unification, where the binary elements of resistance and contemplation, the kingdom and the secular city, redemption and suffering come together. Yet in an attempt to see the oneness of things, Douglass first reinforces a dualism of contrasting elements.

Douglass's dualism is most apparent in the division of truth and untruth, the kingdom versus illusion. One either participates in truth, or one rejects the living truth and lives in illusion. The world is either moving towards the apocalyptic vision of the Kingdom of God or the world is moving towards its own demise. He writes about the choice between two end-times: one holy, one profane. Nonviolence is, of course, the movement towards the kingdom, while violence is the means to dehumanization and destruction.

Douglass's binary division of human action is betrayed in the title of one of his books, "Lightning East to West." The lightning of the violent end of the world, manifested in the H-bomb, stands in opposition to the "lightning East to West" of the nonviolent Kingdom of God. As Douglass writes: "The exact opposite of the H-bomb's destructive purpose, but psychic equivalent of its energy, is the kingdom of Reality which would be the final victory of Truth in history."[1] While agreeing with his sentiment, we may rightly question the parity of these two terms. Does the lightning of God's victory really reduce to a divine H-bomb? Does this not place the Creator on par with the creation, as if God were an object among others? And finally, does not the contemplative's awakening disclose precisely otherwise, that God, far from being an object of our experience is rather the mystery in Whom we live, move, and have our being? Because the gospel cannot be the psychic equivalent of any created thing, it subverts any attempt at dualism. To be fair, Douglass may know this, but his rhetoric fails to do this vision justice.

Douglass's dualistic tone does serve a purpose when one considers his historical context. Speaking to "Milieu-Catholicism" and its muddling of right and wrong, Douglass uses binary logic to force the Church to recognize its complicity in injustice and structural evil. Such dualistic thinking, however, runs aground when it meets with the reality of a muddled right and wrong. This becomes especially clear in Douglass's critique of technique, which he views as a rational and artificial construct that dehumanizes for the sake of efficiency and is therefore, a sin.[2] One would be hard-pressed to assert, however, that a society larger than a few local family units could survive without some form of technique. Abstraction, and to some extent, dehumanization, is necessary to the governance and order of large population centers. This may say something about the massive sizes of our nation-states, but it also reveals that human actions may not be so easily divided between the evil of self-interested power and a pure love of every creature. While I personally find the grasping for political power by environmental and human rights organizations rather disconcerting, their absence in the halls of governance would be even more troublesome.

1. Douglass, *Lightning East to West*, 39.
2. See Douglass, "On Transcending Technique," 50.

These dualistic tendencies seem at odds with Douglass's vision of ontological nonviolence. After all, the vision that reality at its deepest roots is a non-competitive realm of peace ought to subvert our visions of agonistic dualisms. Moreover, one of the fundamental achievements of twentieth-century nonviolence has been the recognition that in any conflictual situation there are more than two courses of action. We do not choose between passive acquiescence and violent conflict, but as Gandhi, Merton, King, and Douglass have all taught us, we seek to find through God creative resolutions, invisible to the binary imagination.

The Problem of Abstraction

Just as Douglass reverts to dualisms to clarify his thought and make a stronger impact on the reader, he also employs a great deal of abstract language for the same reason. Part of the problem is simply the nature of the beast: it is difficult to systematize contemplation and experiences of divine Truth, especially when writing for a popular audience. Additionally, nonviolence itself eludes formulae. As Douglass himself points out, how one adheres to the truth through nonviolence depends on the specific circumstances. To decide what powers must be resisted, for example, requires a selfless wisdom that must be applied to a concrete situation. In an effort to make the abstractions more real, Douglass provides examples from his own life, as well as the lives of Gandhi, Danilo Dolci, Dorothy Day, Cesar Chavez, and many others, whose embrace of nonviolence give substance to his thought.

Nevertheless, Douglass's abstractions make the practical application of his thought problematic. For all of his emphasis on contemplation, Douglass leaves his reader wondering how precisely one contemplates in such a way that one empties the self and is "reduced to zero." What precisely does an emptied self *look* like, and how does one attain it? Douglass's entire argument hinges on a proper understanding of what he intends with terms such as truth, reality, and ego-crucifixion, but we need a fuller account of what this proper understanding is. Let us take an example from his work *Lightning East to West*: "Behind each of those truths of the Gospel which introduces us into a new reality lies an ego-crucifixion of the person Jesus who first passed into that reality. The same baptism by fire is required of us to discover the kingdom's reality today."[3] The truths of the Gospel are hardly uniformly agreed upon among Christians, yet Douglass never precisely details what such truths might be. How do we adhere to Truth

---

3. Douglass, *Lightning East to West*, 3.

outside of our own culturally-defined understanding of such? His abstraction allows the reader to bring his or her own preconceived understanding of truth into Douglass's train of thought, ideas which may eventually undermine Douglass's entire nonviolent project.

Like Truth, the 'Way,' emerges as a key term in *Resistance and Contemplation,* and the 1972 article "Prison." Douglass's use of the term borders on the mystical:

> The Way of sun and shadow reached in and touched me at the center, and when I looked closely was all of the valley withdrawing into darkness again. I knew the Way as giving itself in the deepest silence. No one ever referred to it. The name 'Way' came later as I realized I was walking in it. . . .[4]

The Way, which to Douglass reveals the liberating power of nonviolence, remains obscure. Is there an objective Way apart from one's own subjective spiritual experience? Such questions may be best left to the spiritual masters of the world's religious traditions, but without answers to them, Douglass's assertions about the ontology of nonviolence and its manifestation in the world remain clouded in speculation.

The Problem of Suffering

Before we can critique Douglass's emphasis on suffering, we must begin by again considering his context. In the face of nuclear destruction, Douglass was highly critical of the Church's refusal to tear itself from political alliances and take a conscientious stand against nuclear weapons and the Vietnam War. As Douglass writes, the "Council can be seen as having fallen short of the witness demanded by Christ."[5] Very few Christians, even within the peace movement, were willing to compromise their security and privilege for the sake of those suffering from war and poverty in the Third World. Deeply bothered by the unrecognized and unrepented guilt of the church, with its emphasis on Christ the archetypal hero over Christ the suffering servant, Douglass called Christians to return to the truth of the cross. By neglecting the cross, he asserted, we are unable to realize the kingdom of God, which is the coming of God in nonviolent, suffering love. The importance of the cross, therefore, cannot be underestimated.

Douglass also spoke in accord with liberation theologians who wanted to reclaim the true meaning of the cross—not as a tool of forced acqui-

---

4. Douglass, "Prison," 52.
5. Douglass, *The Non-Violent Cross*, 127.

escence and moralized compliance in the hands of the powerful, but as a voice of freedom realized through struggle and commitment.[6] Douglass emphasizes suffering in order to change its image as a passive acceptance of evil to a powerful and holy means of resistance. He certainly was not alone in this effort. As Klaus Wengst wrote:

> It is no coincidence that this line has been discovered and is being taken up in Latin American liberation theology and black theology. . . . In their own orientation on the cross of Christ, in deliberate acceptance of the suffering that is forced on them, there begins a process of creative liberation which seeks not just conversion but true humanity for the oppressed, and sisterhood and brotherhood for all.[7]

The intensity with which Douglass focuses on suffering and the cross should therefore be considered in light of his intended audience. Even with this in mind, however, Douglass's emphasis on suffering risks misinterpretation. I concur with Charles Curran who, in his book *American Catholic Social Ethics: Twentieth-Century Approaches*, critiques Douglass for too great an emphasis on the Cross.[8] Suffering is so predominant in Douglass's works that one often needs reminding that suffering, in itself, is evil. Suffering alone is not inherently redemptive; love willing to suffer is the force of nonviolent redemption. Any thorough treatment of the value of suffering love needs to be balanced with a significant recognition of the terror of suffering. In the realm of voluntary suffering, one must also distinguish between suffering borne out of love and the self-imposed suffering of self-deprecation and guilt-based penance.

Douglass's emphasis on suffering also threatens to overshadow other aspects of his ontology of nonviolence. Again, Douglass's emphasis on suffering reminds a complacent and comfortable church that "there is no vision of resurrection which is not also a personal invitation to the cross."[9] Yet with such an intense focus on the absolute necessity of suffering, the significance of resurrection can sometimes appear inconsequential. As Curran writes, "the Cross alone is not a symbol of the total reality of Jesus. There is not only the Cross but also the resurrection. Those who have been

---

6. For more on the reclamation of the crucifix, see Robert McAfee Brown, *Gustavo Gutierrez: An Introduction to Liberation Theology* (Maryknoll, NY: Orbis Books, 1990).

7. Klaus Wengst, *Humility: Solidarity of the Humiliated*, trans. John Bowden (Philadelphia: Fortress Press, 1988), 59.

8. See Charles E. Curran, *American Catholic Social Ethics: Twentieth-Century Approaches* (Notre Dame: University of Notre Dame Press, 1982).

9. Douglass, *Resistance and Contemplation: The Way of Liberation*, 45.

Conclusion

baptized into Christ Jesus now truly share in the newness of the life of the resurrection."[10] While Douglass's reader is made aware that there is no resurrection without the cross, it is less apparent from reading his works that the final result of the cross, resurrection, has enormous value in itself.

Curran also critiques Douglass's emphasis on paradox: power in weakness, joy in sorrow, life in death. While his use of paradox serves his emphasis on suffering, Douglass does not allow for a non-paradoxical relationship of the world to God. Curran importantly points out, "Sometimes God's love is known and manifested in human love, God's beauty in human beauty, God's power in human power."[11] While Douglass clearly believes in a sacramental universe, his emphasis on paradox seems to imply that such sacramentality is only realized in opposites. This fails to recognize the power of non-suffering love, worship, and creation in the movement towards God. God's presence has been revealed to humankind not only in experiences of suffering and powerlessness, but in the joys of blessing and fulfillment.

In *The Non-Violent Cross*, for example, Douglass juxtaposes creation, seen as the process of self-discovery and maturation of humankind in this world, with crucifixion, seen as suffering union with God. While both are important to the fulfillment of humanity, Douglass asserts that our self-identity is found not in creation, but in crucifixion.[12] Although mystical theology has traditionally believed purgation, and its concomitant suffering, to be a necessary prerequisite for divine union, Douglass seems to center on crucifixion to the neglect of union. The stripping of the false self must be matched by the building of the True Self. Suffering, while important, should not overwhelm the many means God provides to move us toward the fullness of our humanity in Christ.

As we have seen, Douglass's tendencies towards dualism, abstraction, and the over-valorization of suffering may at times obscure his central vision of ontological nonviolence. Nonetheless, these criticisms are offered not in opposition to but in the service of Douglass's larger project. And indeed, the value of Douglass's project cannot be underestimated. Although this book has set Douglass's ideas within the influence of certain historical trajectories, we must certainly recognize that the relevance of this spiritually-integrated and ontological understanding of nonviolence transcends the confines of a few decades. This is fortunate, as a renewed

---

10. Curran, *American Catholic Social Ethics*, 276.
11. Ibid., 277.
12. Douglass, *The Non-Violent Cross*, 26.

exploration of nonviolence seems only too urgent for our contemporary situation. Recognizing this urgency, this rest of this chapter will look to the ways in which Douglass's ontological theology of nonviolence speaks to the broader forms of violence which confront our society today.

A Renewed Nonviolence

In his book, *Lightning East to West,* Douglass remarks on a small event that occurred in the Fall of 1974:

> *The Bulletin of Atomic Scientists,* a periodical begun after World War II by scientists anxious to avert a nuclear holocaust, moved the hands on its symbolic doomsday clock three minutes closer to midnight—to nine minutes to twelve. . . . Due to a host of historical factors—global famine, injustice, and terrorism; failure of the Strategic Arms Limitation Talks, continued development of nuclear weapons systems, India's first atomic test, Britain's renewal of testing, worldwide proliferation of nuclear technology—and most of all, due to a pervasive sense of the inevitable, deepening violence at the heart of our human spirit in the nuclear age, people everywhere could recognize the truth that we only have a few minutes left.[13]

Almost thirty-three years later, in January of 2007, *The Bulletin of Atomic Scientists* moved the doomsday clock to five minutes to midnight, two minutes closer than in 2002. Although the nuclear risk seemed to diminish in the early 1990s, recent historical events, oddly similar to those mentioned by Douglass, have pressed the scientists to again move the clock steadily forward, events such as nuclear threats between India and Pakistan and the continued development of nuclear weapons in the West as well as in previously nuclear-free countries such as North Korea and Iran. Yet the 2007 clock stands out from the previous fifty years in the recognition of a different problem: for the first time the bulletin attended directly to the threat of climate change and environmental degradation.

To the nuclear threat, the continued use of military action rather than diplomacy, and the economic exploitation of the two-thirds world, Douglass's theology of nonviolence continues to serve as a prophetic call to conversion. One could even argue that the need to hear this call is greater in the twenty-first century than it was just thirty years ago. The great voices that spurred Douglass—Gandhi, Merton, and Day—have been set away in libraries, their lived example only remembered by a few. Martin Luther King, Jr., another influence on Douglass and one of the greatest American

---

13. Douglass, *Lightning East to West,* 57.

proponents of nonviolence, who issued loud warnings against militarization and nuclear proliferation, has in many ways been co-opted by the American government and civil society as a temperate voice for political correctness. The left, as well as the right, struggles to reconcile religion to an ungrounded and often opportunistic sense of politics. The generation that was born into the "hopelessness" of the '70s seems to experience ingrained apathy as a natural response in the face of powerlessness.

Thus, Douglass's articulation of nonviolence remains as valuable, indeed vital, today as it did in previous decades. It calls us to live the Kingdom, to confront the violence that is a continuation of those "untruths" which Douglass dealt with in the latter half of the twentieth century: economic imperialism, war, torture, racism, and an ever-increasing gap between the rich and poor, to name a few. But what of that slow violence that *The Bulletin of Atomic Scientists* recently recognized as a danger nearly as grave as nuclear weapons—the problem of climate change and damaged ecosystems? What might an ontology of nonviolence say to this more subtle, and therefore potentially more venomous form of violence—a violence inflicted on creation that reverberates back onto humanity?[14]

At first glance, nonviolence may not seem appropriate, or even relevant to the challenge of ecological devastation. One might argue that even if it were possible for humans to act violently towards non-humans (a concession that is by no means a given in contemporary conversation), only top-down legal and political change can enforce a more "acceptable use" of creation's resources. Indeed, the challenge of climate change presents no single enemy to be confronted, no single institutional act to be protested. The victim is not in a position to win the oppressor's heart with suffering love. That which must be resisted is not outside of ourselves, in some separate institution of governance or economic structure. Indeed, as Wendell Berry has said, "Nearly every one of us, nearly every day of his life, is contributing directly to the ruin of this planet. A protest meeting on the issue of environmental abuse is not a convocation of accusers, it is a convocation of the guilty."[15]

Yet it is precisely here we may begin to see why an ontology of nonviolence, particularly as it is articulated by Douglass, presents a vision and

---

14. Here we must recognize that Douglass, Day, Gandhi, and Merton all recognized ecological degradation as a form of violence deeply connected with the exploitation of the poor and the militarization of society. I believe this offers further support for the relevance of a nonviolent ontology to the larger human situation.

15. Wendell Berry, "Think Little," in *A Continuous Harmony: Essays Cultural and Agricultural* (New York: Harcourt Brace Jovanovich, 1972), 72.

call capable of answering today's broader forms of violence, including the structural violence of environmental degradation. As Douglass emphasizes, an ontology of nonviolence requires that we begin with ourselves first and foremost, for "as you are, so is the world." This points us to those more intimate forms of violence that live as much in the human heart and its habits as in the world. Therefore, let us take a closer look at the relevance of an ontology of nonviolence for the environmental crisis before us.

A nonviolent posture stands in contrast to the current response towards "solving" climate change and environmental abuse. The focus of the current discussion has largely centered on enhanced "green technologies" that are implemented on a global scale—wind and solar power, biofuels, and hydrogen cars are among those mentioned most often. While I applaud the expansion of these needed technologies, the techno-economic approach to solving the environmental crisis remains primarily one of merely managing our violence towards, and exploitation of, creation. Because decision-makers and many of their constituencies commonly assume that the real challenge before us is the development of less destructive technologies, it is also assumed that we in the West can continue to live with the same levels of security, comfort, and control that we have enjoyed for the last few decades, perhaps centuries. Thus our relationship with creation can remain one largely mediated by market-forces, with the worth of creation directly dependent upon how efficiently it provides for human desire.

As we have seen, a posture of nonviolence, on the other hand, asserts a profound relationship between the way we arrive at a desired end and the end itself. It involves witnessing to the truth in the very way we live and realizing the Kingdom in our resistance to unjust and exploitative practices. As Douglass insists, the cross of suffering love is a necessary component of this adherence to the ways of the Kingdom. The "downward mobility" that accompanies the movement towards a more just, sustainable, and ecologically-cooperative society may seem painful and hard to accept. And it must be admitted that there is certainly a level of suffering in accepting the limits of resource use, sharing wealth, taking the longer and less 'efficient' route away from disposability, and accepting sacrifices of privilege, comfort, and security. Yet when willingly endured for the love of God's creation and the poor who are always the most victimized by environmental exploitation, we align ourselves, as Douglass would say, with the way of the Kingdom.

What has been described is not necessarily nonviolent, however, as there are extant environmental ethics that makes similar demands while at the same time encouraging the fragmentation, conflict, and dehumanization that drive power politics. Like the peace movement that confronts the endless temptation to transform the world from the 'outside,' the environmental movement perhaps suffers even more from a deontological ethic. The real contribution of an ontology of nonviolence is the recognition that at root, the ravaging of creation requires us to respond not so much in terms of duty or with utilitarian gumshoe, as with spiritual transformation. The crisis before us, like the accumulation of weapons, is borne of a personal and collective ego-attachment that masks an inner emptiness. The violence enacted towards creation is a continuation of those historical cycles of violence understood so well by Douglass that protect the security and power of the illusory self. We buttress our vulnerable selves with the assurance of hubris, control, and material accumulation. The shelter of hubris is our unwillingness to confront a world of limits, an inexhaustible confidence that the scientific mind can free us of discomfort, death, and dependency. It is this fear of dependency that we mask with delusions of control. Control—that sigh of relief when I can tell myself that I depend on nothing. To depend on the providence of God is to be vulnerable, and it is much more pleasant to place my confidence in the promises of production, economic growth, and the accumulation of wealth.

As Douglass maintains, nonviolence as an ontological reality requires *metanoia*. This conversion must come from the contemplation of my own emptiness and the emptiness of my collective human family. With this contemplation comes the stark realization that improved technologies may not release us from experiencing the dire consequences of climate change. Such contemplation reveals, too, our own individual powerlessness in the face of a suffering creation. All of my individual attempts at living sustainably will not change a destructive human society. Yet, this is the true liberation: to live in a way that responds to a suffering world because in love there is no other choice. As Douglass writes, "This is not a question of whether or not I am able to resist, or whether or not I should. In the age of genocide to be human is to resist."[16] To be human is to resist the genocide of creation inasmuch as I am able, forgoing the illusion of control, and trusting that God is present there.

This is profoundly different from the existential response, borne out of despair, that haunts the environmental movement. A nonviolent response is not merely a question of personal integrity because contemplation releases us to act, not according to our own will, but according to the goodness of God's Kingdom. Contemplation allows us to be vulnerable

16. Douglass, *Resistance and Contemplation*, 141.

enough to love and appreciate the inherent value of that which is not ourselves, that which is perhaps not even human. Through nonviolence, we are released of our need for a successful outcome, allowing us to be absorbed into the means, where our hope lies not in our own capacities but in a Kingdom that we can never manipulate. Ontological nonviolence gives us reason beyond duty or utility to live in comportment to the Good. We trust that our actions participate in the advent of the Kingdom that is never absent. Our actions are not subject to the calculus of return, but are obscurely already a part of God's recreation of this world.

Thankfully, one of the greatest gifts we have in knowing the ontological presence of God is creation itself. For all who have found themselves vulnerable in the wilderness, who have seen its value completely independent of any human 'use' will, like Douglass in the sunlit valley or Merton in the rain, know intimately the Reality that brings us back to our true selves, the Reality that calls us to the Kingdom here, waiting.

So where do we go from here? The wedding of resistance and contemplation—a modern variant on the age old question of contemplation and action, of Mary's one thing needful and Martha's buzz of activity—still beckons. Douglass's writings suggest a number of theoretical solutions that can be helpful in the continuing realization of the kingdom's coming and should be a resource for activists and contemplatives for years to come. But more important even than Douglass's theory is the lived experience from which his theory is born. Douglass is always calling his readers to do more than ponder these matters—he calls us to live them. The theology of Cross and Kingdom and the ontology of nonviolence are completed by a response of a radical commitment to the nonviolent reality of God, to contemplative resistance, on the part of the reader. This is a text that Douglass could not write for it can only be inscribed in lives committed to love and justice, and open to an incarnate political witness that remains at the same time a prayer.

Bibliography

Human Life in Our Day: A Collective Pastoral Letter of the American Hierarchy. Issued November 15, 1968. Washington, D. C.: the Conference, 1968.
Resolution on Southeast Asia: November, 1971. Washington, D. C.: United States Catholic Conference, 1971.
Amato, Joseph. *Mounier and Maritain: A French Catholic Understanding of the Modern World.* University: University of Alabama Press, 1975.
Amery, Carl. *Capitulation: The Lesson of German Catholicism.* Translated by Edward Quinn. New York: Herder and Herder, 1967.
Anderson, George M. "Believing in the Miracle of Peace: An Interview with James Douglass." *America* February 26, 2007, 17–20.
Berry, Wendell. "Think Little." In *A Continuous Harmony: Essays Cultural & Agricultural.* New York: Harcourt Brace Jovanovich, 1972.
Bonhoeffer, Dietrich. *Letters and Papers from Prison.* Edited by Eberhard Bethge. New York: Macmillan, 1962.
Boyer, Paul. *By the Bomb's Early Light: American Thought and Culture at the Dawn of the Atomic Age.* Chapel Hill: University of North Carolina Press, 1994.
Brown, Robert McAfee. *Gustavo Gutierrez: An Introduction to Liberation Theology.* Maryknoll, NY: Orbis Books, 1990.
Callahan, Annice. *Spiritual Guides for Today.* New York: Crossroad, 1992.
Catholic Bishops of the United States. "Religion, Our Most Vital National Asset." *Catholic Action* 34, no. 12 (1952): 3–5, 20.
Chernus, Ira. *American Nonviolence: The History of an Idea.* Maryknoll, NY: Orbis Books, 2004.
Chinnici, Joseph P. "The Catholic Community at Prayer, 1926–1976." In *Habits of Devotion: Catholic Religious Practice in Twentieth-Century America*, edited by James M. O'Toole, 8–87. Ithaca: Cornell University Press, 2004.
Chinnici, Joseph P., and Angelyn Dries, eds. *Prayer and Practice in the American Catholic Community.* Edited by Christopher J. Kauffman, *American Catholic Identies: A Documentary History.* Maryknoll, NY: Orbis Books, 2000.
Curran, Charles E. *American Catholic Social Ethics: Twentieth-Century Approaches.* Notre Dame: University of Notre Dame Press, 1982.
Dalton, Dennis, ed. *Mahatma Gandhi: Selected Political Writings.* Indianapolis: Hackett Publishing Company, Inc., 1996.
Day, Dorothy. *The Long Loneliness: The Autobiography of Dorothy Day.* San Francisco: Harper San Francisco, 1997.
———. *On Pilgrimage.* New York: Catholic Worker Books, 1948.
Dohen, Dorothy. *Nationalism and American Catholicism.* New York: Sheed and Ward, Inc., 1967.
Dougherty, James E. *The Bishops and Nuclear Weapons.* Hamden, CT: Archon Books, 1984.

Bibliography

Douglass, James W. "Civil Disobedience as Prayer." In *Swords into Plowshares: Nonviolent Direct Action for Disarmament, Peace, Social Justice*, edited by Arthur J. Laffin and Anne Montgomery. Marion, SD: Fortkamp Publishing, 1996.

———. *Lightning East to West: Jesus, Gandhi, and the Nuclear Age*. New York: Crossroad Publishing Company, 1983. Reprint, with a new afterword by John Dear, Eugene, OR: Wipf & Stock, 2006.

———. "The Negative Theology of Dionysius the Areopagite." *The Downside Review*, no. 81 (1963): 115–24.

———. "Non-Violence and Metanoia." *Katallagete* 5, no. 2 (1974): 28–31.

———. *The Non-Violent Cross*. New York: The Macmillan Company, 1968. Reprint, with a new forward by Ched Myers, Eugene, OR: Wipf & Stock, 2006.

———. *The Nonviolent Coming of God*. Maryknoll, NY: Orbis Books, 1993. Reprint, with a new forward by Jonathan Wilson-Hartgrove, Eugene, OR: Wipf & Stock, 2006.

———. "On Transcending Technique." *Katallagete*, Winter (1970): 49–51.

———. "Prison." *Katallagete* (1972): 51–54.

———. *Resistance and Contemplation: The Way of Liberation*. Garden City, NY: Doubleday & Company, Inc., 1972. Reprint, with a new foreword by Elizabeth McAlister, Eugene, OR: Wipf & Stock, 2006.

———. "Resistance, Contemplation, Liberation." *Katallagete*, Spring (1971): 13–20.

———. "Thomas Merton's Glimpse of the Kingdom." In *The Message of Thomas Merton*, edited by Patrick Hart, 204–10. Kalamazoo: Cistercian Publications, 1981.

Echols, Alice. "Nothing Distant About It: Women's Liberation and Sixties Radicalism." In *The Sixties: From Memory to History*, edited by David Farber, 149–74. Chapel Hill: The University of North Carolina Press, 1994.

Ellsberg, Robert, ed. *By Little and by Little: The Selected Writings of Dorothy Day*. New York: Alfred A. Knopf, 1984.

———, ed. *Dorothy Day: Selected Writings*. Maryknoll, NY: Orbis Books, 2002.

Ellul, Jacques. *The Technological Society*. Translated by John Wilkinson. New York: Alfred A. Knopf, 1965.

Farber, Beth Bailey and David, ed. *America in the Seventies*. Lawrence, KS: University Press of Kansas, 2004.

Farber, David. "Introduction." In *The Sixties*, edited by David Farber, 1–10. Chapel Hill: North Carolina University Press, 1994.

Flannery, Austin, ed. *Vatican Council II, the Conciliar and Post Conciliar Documents*. New rev. ed, *Vatican Collection; V. 1*. Collegeville, Ind.: Liturgical Press, 1992.

Flannery, Harry W., ed. *Patterns for Peace: Catholic Statements on International Order*. Westminster, MD: Newman, 1962.

Gandhi, M. K. *Non-Violent Resistance*. New York: Schocken Books, 1961.

Gandhi, Mahatma. *The Collective Works of Mahatma Gandhi*. Vol. 38. Delhi: Publications Division, Ministry of Information and Broadcasting, Government of India, 1958–94.

———. *God Is Truth*. Edited by Anand T. Hingorani. [2d] ed. Bombay: Bharatiya Vidya Bhavan, 1962.

Gibbons, William J. *Pacem in Terris. Peace on Earth; Encyclical Letter of His Holiness Pope John XXIII*. New York: Paulist Press, 1963.

Givey, David W. *The Social Thought of Thomas Merton: The Way of Nonviolence and Peace for the Future*. Chicago: Franciscan Herald Press, 1983.

Hauerwas, Stanley. *With the Grain of the Universe: The Church's Witness and Natural Theology: Being Gifford Lectures Delivered at the University of St. Andrews in 2001*. Grand Rapids, MI: Brazos Press, 2001.

Bibliography

Hayes, Carlton Joseph Huntley. *Patriotism, Nationalism and the Brotherhood of Man; a Report of the Committee on National Attitudes, [Catholic Association for International Peace] Pamphlet; No. 25.* [New York: Paulist Press], 1937.

Hehir, J. Bryan. "The Just-War Ethic and Catholic Theology: Dynamics of Change and Continuity." In *War or Peace? The Search for New Answers*, edited by Thomas A. Shannon, 15–39. Maryknoll, NY: Orbis Books, 1982.

Holben, Lawrence. *All the Way to Heaven: A Theological Reflection on Dorothy Day, Peter Maurin, and the Catholic Worker.* Marion, SD: Rose Hill Books, 1997.

Iyer, Raghavan, ed. *The Essential Writings of Mahatma Gandhi.* New Delhi: Oxford University Press, 2004.

Kripalani, J. B. *Gandhi: His Life and Thought.* Delhi: Publications Division, Ministry of Information and Broadcasting, Government of India, 1971.

Lammers, Stephen E. "Catholic Ethics and Pacifism." In *War or Peace? The Search for New Answers*, edited by Thomas A. Shannon, 93–103. Maryknoll, NY: Orbis Books, 1982.

McDonnell, Thomas P., ed. *A Thomas Merton Reader.* New York, 1962.

McNeal, Patricia F. *The American Catholic Peace Movement.* New York: Arno Press, 1978.

Merriman, Brigid O'Shea. *Searching for Christ: The Spirituality of Dorothy Day.* Notre Dame, IN: University of Notre Dame Press, 1994.

Merton, Thomas. *The Asian Journal of Thomas Merton.* Edited by Patrick Hart Naomi Burton, and James Laughlin. New York: New Directions Publishing, 1973.

———. *Contemplation in a World of Action.* Notre Dame, IN: University of Notre Dame Press, 1998.

———. *Faith and Violence: Christian Teaching and Christian Practice.* Notre Dame, IN: University of Notre Dame Press, 1994.

———. *The Hidden Ground of Love.* Edited by William H. Shannon. New York: Farrar, Straus, Giroux, 1985.

———. *Mystics and Zen Masters.* New York: Farrar, Straus, & Giroux, 1967.

———. *New Seeds of Contemplation.* New York: New Directions, 1972.

———. *The Nonviolent Alternative.* Edited by Gordon C. Zahn. New York: Farrar, Straus, and Giroux, 1980.

———. *Seeds of Destruction.* New York: Farrar, Straus, and Giroux, 1964.

———. *The Seven Storey Mountain.* 50th anniversary ed. New York: Harcourt Brace, 1998.

———. *Zen and the Birds of Appetite, A New Directions Book.* [New York: New Directions, 1968.

Merton, Thomas, and William Henry Shannon. *The Hidden Ground of Love: The Letters of Thomas Merton on Religious Experience and Social Concerns.* New York: Farrar, Straus, Giroux, 1985.

Mott, Michael. *The Seven Mountains of Thomas Merton.* Boston: Houghton Mifflin, 1984.

Musto, Ronald G. *The Catholic Peace Tradition.* Maryknoll, NY: Orbis Books, 1986.

National Conference of Catholic Bishops. *The Challenge of Peace: God's Promise and Our Response.* East Orange, N.J.: Advocate Pub. Corp., 1983.

O'Brien, David J. "American Catholic Opposition to the Vietnam War: A Preliminary Assessment." In *War or Peace? The Search for New Answers*, edited by Thomas A. Shannon, 119–50. Maryknoll, NY: Orbis Books, 1982.

Piehl, Mel. *Breaking Bread: The Catholic Worker and the Origin of Catholic Radicalism in America.* Philadelphia: Temple University Press, 1982.

Pozzetta, David R. Colburn and George E. "Race, Ethnicity, and the Evolution of Political Legitimacy." In *The Sixties: From Memory to History*, edited by David Farber, 119–48. Chapel Hill: The University of North Carolina Press, 1994.

Bibliography

Preston, Kenneth. "Seeking the Reign of God: James Douglass' Theology of Nonviolence." MA Thesis, Graduate Theological Union, 2001.
Shannon, William H., ed. *The Hidden Ground of Love: The*, 1985.
Smith, Matthew R. "The Catholic Worker Movement: Toward a Theology of Liberation for First World Disciples." In *Dorothy Day and the Catholic Worker Movement: Centenary Essays*, edited by Phillip Runkel William Thorn, Susan Mountin. Milwaukee: Marquette University Press, 2001.
Statnick, Roger A. "Dorothy Day: Citizen of the Kingdom." In *Dorothy Day and the Catholic Worker Movement: Centenary Essays*, edited by Phillip Runkel, William Thorn, Susan Mountin. Milwaukee: Marquette University Press, 2001.
Thorn, William, Phillip Runkel, and Susan Mountin, eds. *Dorothy Day and the Catholic Worker Movement: Centenary Essays*. Milwaukee: Marquette University Press, 2001.
Wengst, Klaus. *Humility: Solidarity of the Humiliated*. Translated by John Bowden. Philadelphia: Fortress Press, 1988.
Wolpert, Stanley A. *Gandhi's Passion: The Life and Legacy of Mahatma Gandhi*. New York: Oxford University Press, 2001.